MURDER MOST GROTESQUE

MURDER MOST GROTESQUE

The Comedic Crime Fiction of Joyce Porter

CHRIS CHAN

LEVEL
BEST BOOKS

As always, to my parents, Carlyle and Patricia Chan.
And to Martin Edwards, for his advice and encouragement.

Contents

List of Title Abbreviations

Dover Books

Dover One: *D1*

Dover Two: *D2*

Dover Three: *D3*

Dover and the Unkindest Cut of All: *DUCA*

Dover Goes to Pott: *DGP*

Dover Strikes Again: *DSA*

It's Murder with Dover: *IMD*

Dover and the Claret Tappers: *DCT*

Dead Easy for Dover: *DED*

Dover Beats the Band: *DBB*

Dover: The Collected Short Stories: *DCSS*

Dover and the Deadly Poison Pen Letters (Television adaptation title of *Dover Two*): *DDPPL*

Dover and the Sleeping Beauty (Radio adaptation title of *Dover Two*): *DSB*

Dover and the Smoking Gun (Original radio play): *DSG*

Eddie Brown Books

Sour Cream with Everything: *SCE*

The Chinks in the Curtain: *CC*

Neither a Candle Nor a Pitchfork: *NCNP*

Only with a Bargepole: *OB*

Hon Con Books

Introduction

The World of Joyce Porter

Joyce Porter wrote mystery novels with detectives that readers could love while simultaneously having absolutely no confidence in their ability to solve crimes. Porter created three series and became a bestselling author around the world thanks to her twisty plots, outrageous humor, and entertainingly grotesque characters.

Her most famous detective, DCI Wilfrid Dover, is a sluggish, foul-tempered, obese homicide investigator with terrible personal hygiene and gastrointestinal problems. When his bosses at Scotland Yard force him to investigate a murder, he devotes as much time as he can get away with to consuming vast quantities of food and alcohol and interviewing as few suspects as possible. Yet due to amazing luck and occasional flashes of inspiration, Dover manages to catch a surprising number of killers.

In a quartet of comic espionage thrillers, Eddie Brown was a secret agent who hated his job. Dragged into the spy world against his will, Eddie was far better at whining than following orders. Forced to perform a series of increasingly humiliating missions, Eddie tried to help England win the Cold War, yet repeatedly succeeded only in causing terrible messes and getting himself in inescapable situations.

Finally, the Honorable Constance Morrison-Burke, known to all behind her back as the "Hon Con," was a titled lady of mature years who believed herself to be a natural private investigator. Filled with unquenchable self-confidence and determination, the Hon Con threw herself body and soul into her cases, even when the police begged her not to get involved. Parsimonious despite her wealth, oblivious to the scorn and ridicule the community directed towards her, and an essentially out-of-the-closet lesbian, the Hon Con always unraveled the truth...though the authorities would often punish her for her successful yet often destructive efforts.

After learning about her mysteries, the intrigued reader of this critical study might wonder, what do we know about the author herself? The answer is, not much. Some crime writers are as mysterious as their books. Aside from a few extremely brief blurbs on the covers or opening and closing pages of her novels, virtually all the published autobiographical details about her life come from a short biographical essay written by her brother The Reverend Canon J.R. Porter, which was published at the end of *DCS*.

Porter was born in 1924 in a village with a perfect name for a future mystery writer—Marple—in the county of Cheshire, in the northwestern region of England (Back cover flap). Porter would later base many of the settings, weather events, and characters of her books in part on her experiences from her hometown. Porter's education consisted of church elementary school, followed by a scholarship to defray high school expenses, capped off by an English degree at London's King's College, and she worked in the women's branch of the army in the final years of WWII. After briefly-held jobs in secretarial positions, Porter would eventually sign up for work in the Women's Royal Air Force in 1949, where she learned Russian, and spent the next twelve years serving her nation through espionage during the Cold War.

Unfortunately for curious fans, even Porter's family never learned exactly what her work entailed, and any adventures she might have had are hidden from the public, probably guarded under the Official Secrets Act. It is safe to assume that her work did inspire the Eddie Brown novels and the Russia-set Hon Con book *PIM*. When her bosses transferred her to recruitment work, Porter, who had previously adored her job, grew restless and retired from her first major career in 1963 (290).

Her family was initially nervous when Porter proclaimed that she was becoming a mystery writer, but when she left the world of spycraft she had already completed the first three Dover novels and had them accepted by a publisher. *D1* debuted in 1963, and for the next seventeen years, Porter would produce at least one book a year, crafted by working four hours daily, seven days a week. Though she is known for her humor, she once quipped, "Personally, I wouldn't read a funny detective story if you paid me" (291). Porter declared, "I have one virtue as a writer. Once I've started a book, I finish it. Always." (293) Porter soon built up a loyal following, and eventually produced twenty novels and several short stories that would be anthologized posthumously. She stated that for a crime writer to be successful, it was critical "to keep on writing the same story—for a lifetime if necessary—and publish it under different titles" (293).

By 1980, Porter was growing tired of her second career, so she retired from writing mysteries and spent the last decade of her life travelling and researching a biography of the Russian Grand Duchess Elizabeth (295). This biographical project never came into fruition, for Porter passed away in 1990 at the age of sixty-six. She took ill on a trip to Asia and passed away on the plane ride home (296).

As of this writing, there has been no full-length biography of Porter, and it's probable that most of the available information about her professional life and work is classified. Outside of fan blogs, one of the very few published pieces of critical work on Porter is the noted crime author Robert Barnard's introductory essay at the beginning of *DCS*. Barnard's piece is fairly short, and he devotes as much time talking about the corrupt police officer at the center of Joe Orton's infamous play *Loot* as he does to Porter and her creations (1-6). Porter's critical reputation rests as one of the best comedic mystery writers of the twentieth century, though that ignores some of her other strengths, such as characterization in miniature, plotting, and social satire. In his overview of crime fiction *Bloody Murder*, Julian Symons declared that "the post-war period has produced two successful writers of crime comedy." (225) Porter was one, Colin Watson was the other. While Symons spoke highly of *Dover One*, other works and the "Hon Con" did not receive the same level of accolades. Symons's critiques in *Bloody Murder* are notoriously controversial amongst crime fiction fans.

Hopefully, this book will spark more interest in research into a delightful, insightful, and hilarious writer.

I

Part One

Detective Chief Inspector Wilfrid Dover:
Scotland Yard's Laziest and Most Uncouth Sleuth

Wilfred Dover

Wilfrid Dover is in many ways a repellent man. That is what makes him so memorable. Scotland Yard detectives have often come off unflatteringly in mystery fiction. Sir Arthur Conan Doyle, Agatha Christie, and Dorothy L. Sayers created Inspectors Lestrade, Gregson, Japp, and Sugg. All of these fictional detectives are decent and dedicated men, but when compared to the non-official supersleuths like Sherlock Holmes, Hercule Poirot, and Lord Peter Wimsey, the Scotland Yard men invariably come across as hapless and dim, at least when standing in the shadows of the great detectives of fiction. Good, solid men, certainly, but when a particularly difficult case is at hand, mystery fans know that the investigation is best left to the unofficial geniuses.

There are many exceptions, of course. Plenty of prominent crime writers cast an official Scotland Yard detective as their primary sleuth, such as Ngaio Marsh's Inspector Roderick Alleyn. Yet even the most ineffectual fictional Scotland Yard detective was generally portrayed as a salt-of-the-earth fellow at heart. On those rare occasions when Agatha Christie made a police officer the killer, it was particularly surprising, especially amongst the contemporaneous readers of Golden Age detective fiction, to think of such vile behavior in the official force.

Dover is not a villain, but he is unhygienic, selfish, controlling, short-tempered, bullying, gluttonous, stingy, prone to kleptomania, and above all, as lazy as a sloth on sleeping pills. Dover's appearance, first described in *D1*, sets off alarm bells immediately. Obese, clad in a well-worn, badly fitting suit in perpetual need of cleaning, sporting a battered bowler hat, and displaying the kind of moustache that "the late Adolf Hitler did so much to depopularize," Dover is not the sort of fellow who makes it onto the covers of fashion magazines (15). His frequent gastrointestinal upsets, dandruff, and poorly fitting National Health-issued dentures are the stuff of legend.

"Detective Chief Inspector Dover was a big man. His six-foot-two frame was draped, none too elegantly, in seventeen and a quarter stone of flabby flesh, an excessive proportion of which had settled round his middle. Well-cut clothing can, of course, do wonders to conceal such defects as the spread of middle age, but Dover bought his suits ready-made, and the one he was wearing had been purchased a long time ago. It was made of shiny blue serge. Round his thick, policeman's neck he wore a blue-striped collar which was almost submerged in folds of fat, and a thin, cheap tie was knotted under the lowest of his double chins. He wore a long, dark blue overcoat and stout black boots. Over the whole of this unprepossessing ensemble there was, naturally enough, Dover's face. It was large and flabby like the rest of him. Only the details—nose, mouth and eyes—seemed out of scale. They were so tiny as to be almost lost in the wide expanse of flesh. Dover had two small, mean, button-like eyes, a snub little nose and a sulky rosebud of a mouth. He looked like one of those pastry men that children make on baking days out of odd scraps, with currants for eyes—an uncooked pastry man of course" (15).

Dover puts no more interest into his work than he does in his personal appearance. On one occasion, his long-suffering assistant Sergeant Charles Edward MacGregor, notes in *IMD* that Dover's ideal case would involve flipping through the phone book and arresting a name chosen at random (131-132). Dover has a habit of suspecting early and often, considering a swift resolution to the case to be the ideal result, and one arrested suspect is as good as another, justice and actual culpability be damned.

Thankfully, there are no innocent people convicted in the Dover novels, because even though from time to time a guilty party may slip through the long arms of the law, Dover never actually sends the wrong person to prison, despite his frequent urges to make an arrest any way possible. On multiple occasions, Dover muses that he has frequently tried to twist the facts in his career to fit his arrest, but we never see him frame a suspect in any book. On multiple occasions, Dover tries to browbeat, bully, and physically intimidate a suspect into confessing, and sometimes it works, as in *D1*, although a modicum of investigation would have unearthed a plethora of forensic evidence that would have made the third degree unnecessary. The fact that Dover does not cause the conviction of innocent people due to his reluctance to perform a full investigation is not due to pure luck. Dover's assistant, Sergeant MacGregor, wears himself to a nub trying to keep his boss as honest as possible.

MacGregor was partnered with Dover by a micromanaging administrator who believed that young, up-and-coming police officers should be given a kind of trial by fire to acclimate them to the roughest part of the job and to stamp out streaks of arrogance and overconfidence, and MacGregor's training was a partnership with Scotland Yard's most difficult detective. Dover treats MacGregor as his assistant, chauffeur, and general dogsbody. Dover insists that MacGregor pay for all meals and for an endless supply of drinks and cigarettes, which severely depletes MacGregor's income. Dover rarely expresses appreciation for MacGregor's sacrifices, and rudely dismisses most of MacGregor's independent contributions to the investigations and theories, unless Dover can find a way to claim these ideas for his own. Unfortunately for MacGregor, it's revealed in *IMD* (published nine years after *D1*) that being paired with Dover has effectively derailed his career and that his name is now inextricably linked with Dover's. By the midpoint in the series, MacGregor has resigned himself to the fact that Dover's effect on his reputation has killed off any chances of promotion, but he still lives in hope of an eventual transfer, despite the fact that his superiors see him as "useless by association" (115-116). MacGregor is consistently frustrated in his dream because nobody else has any intention of working with Dover.

Despite MacGregor's frustrated loathing for his boss and Dover's unveiled contempt for his underling, the two do make a highly effective investigative team. MacGregor manages to keep Dover in line as much as humanly possible, and between the two of them, they manage to gather up plenty of valuable information. Interestingly, despite his many flaws, Dover is an effective detective, who manages to solve the case through shrewd observations and deductions most of the time, though now and then MacGregor unravels the puzzle, occasionally the pair solves the crime together, and in at least two instances the guilty party confesses spontaneously.

The partnership between Dover and MacGregor, along with MacGregor's very different personality, is summarized early in their first adventure, *D1*.

"Charles Edward MacGregor was, in fact, feeling nearly as hard done by as Dover was, though for a slightly different reason. He regarded himself, and was indeed regarded by his superiors, as one of the up-and-coming young officers at the Yard. He was intelligent, efficient, courteous and sympathetic, and extremely well dressed to boot. It seemed unfair that he should be coupled with Chief Inspector Dover, who was his exact opposite in almost everything. But the Assistant Commissioner, who kept a fatherly eye on these matters, was a great believer in baptisms of fire and salvation through suffering and he frequently used Dover to provide both for young detectives whose opinion of themselves was, perhaps, a little too high. The Assistant Commissioner felt, with some justification, that if a lad could stick Dover, he could stick almost anything. It was damned good character training! He had, therefore, turned a deaf ear to the pleas of both Dover and Sergeant MacGregor that the first case* upon which they had been engaged together should be their last" (13-14).

Dover and MacGregor are a deeply entertaining odd couple, with Dover constantly shocking and offending those around him, and MacGregor constantly humiliated and desperate to keep situations from spiraling out of control. Interestingly, though one may feel sorry for MacGregor at times, the sergeant has plenty of his own flaws. Vain, smug, obsessed with his own good looks and appearance, frequently petulant, and unaware of his own conceited nature, one can understand why the bosses at Scotland Yard decided that MacGregor would benefit from an extended series of lessons on humility. Mac-

Gregor is convinced that he is the proud owner of the finest brain at Scotland Yard, even though his despised superior has far more successfully solved cases on his account, and MacGregor's "hunches" frequently produce no fruitful results. Yet if MacGregor were not so driven and ambitious, Dover would not be so annoyed and fearful of being overshadowed by his subordinate that he makes just enough effort to figure out the identity of the killer. It is implied, though, that the vast majority of Dover's investigations are doomed to failure, and that readers only get to see that small fraction of cases that see a successful conclusion.

Over the course of ten novels and several short stories, Dover and MacGregor investigate cases that reflected the darkest and most twisted aspects of society but always did so with humor and wit. Notably, though the titles of the Hon Con and Eddie Brown novels were distinctive and memorable, many of the Dover titles were completely nondescriptive and interchangeable with any other title, with a few exceptions (*Dover and the Unkindest Cut of All*, *Dover and the Claret Tappers*, and to a lesser extent *Dover Goes to Pott* and *Dover Beats the Band*). When a few titles were published under alternate titles (*Dover Fails to Make His Mark*, *A Terrible Drag for Dover*, *When Dover Gets Knotted*, and *Dover Doesn't Dilly-Dally*), the new titles were no more evocative of the contents of the stories. This is a shame, for the Dover novels are such skillful masterpieces of blended farce and darkness, that the titles really ought to be representative of the cleverness and inventiveness of the original novels.

Each Dover novel is a blend of original plotting, inspired comedy, and social satire. In this section, every Dover novel is summarized, the mystery and clueing are explained (with

8

as few spoilers as possible), and Porter's sly commentary on the state of English society is profiled. Humor and mystery blend to provide marvelous entertainment, as the following chapters will show.

* "Inspector Dover and the Spilt Milk" – this case has not been and will not be published at any price.

Chapter One: Dover One (1964)

The Plot

Dover's first recorded case is one of his darkest and funniest. As the story opens, it develops a template that would serve as a formula for most of the rest of the series. A mysterious crime affects a rural English village, and when the local police decide that they need help to solve the case (or alternatively, want someone else to shoulder the blame if things go wrong), they turn to Scotland Yard in order to investigate. Scotland Yard, which is perpetually short-staffed and has few detectives to ship outside of London, spitefully sends out Detective Chief Inspector Dover, more to get him out of their hair for a while than because they think that he will actually solve the crime.

The dynamic between Dover and MacGregor is established fully formed right from the start. Both men despise the other. MacGregor is perpetually exasperated by Dover's laziness, rudeness, tendency to use violence to intimidate suspects, and voracious consumption of endless quantities of food, alcohol, and cigarettes, all of which are purchased by MacGregor as kind of apprenticeship fee. MacGregor's superiors partnered him with Dover as a form of hazing experience, expecting that dealing with a bit of frustration and adversity would build character in a young detective whose opinion of himself far outstrips his actual abilities. Dover is comparably irked by MacGregor's conceit and superior attitude and even more appalled by MacGregor's expectation that as detectives, they ought to work themselves to the bone in order to actually solve the crime. The mutual contempt never wanes nor is tempered by anything resembling respect or affection. Yet despite their antipathy towards each other, they make a pretty effective crime-solving team, at least in the cases that are recorded for posterity as readers are reminded that on countless occasions, Dover's cases go unsolved.

As *D1* opens, the local constabulary are mystified by the sudden disappearance of Juliet Rugg, a teenager working in a domestic capacity for one of the village's richest residents. Juliet was an unmarried mother, had a reputation for disrespectful behavior, and at just over five feet tall, weighed sixteen stone (two hundred twenty-four pounds). What happened to her? She had nowhere to run away to, was unlikely to have been kidnapped, and did not seem suicidal. But if she was murdered, then where is the body?

The bulk of *D1* consists of a series of interviews between Dover, MacGregor, and the colorful characters that form the list of suspects. As a general rule in a Porter novel, the more comically grotesque the supporting cast, the better the book, and the rogue's gallery that populates the investigation in *D1* is among the best.

Mrs. Rugg, Juliet's mother, has four children by three different fathers and is none too pleased about looking after her grandbaby. Mrs. Chubb-Smith, the unlucky landlady of the housing estate, thought that her son Michael was the father of Juliet's baby, and generously supported her throughout her pregnancy until the child was born, and it turned out to have a father of African heritage. Juliet's employer, Sir John Counter, is a randy and bigoted old satyr who expected his employees to satisfy his sexual needs, and his daughter Eve Counter is a prudish sort who realized that Juliet had an eye on becoming her father's second wife, and may have been being blackmailed by Juliet. Boris Bogolepov is a drug addict living on the dole, claiming to be both gay and a Holocaust survivor, though the truth of both of these assertions is called into question over the course of the investigation.

One of the most likeable characters is Colonel Bing, a boisterous former military woman and dog lover living in an ambiguously lesbian relationship with the kindly yet scatterbrained Miss Georgie McLintock. Colonel Bing and Miss McLintock are likely prototypes for the Hon Con and Miss Jones, and given the obvious enjoyment Porter had creating the Colonel, it's not surprising that she would expand a revised version of her into a recurring detective. Less amiable is Sergeant-Major William Bondy, an ex-military man with a strong dislike of children and pets, and strong opinions about his neighbors. Mr. Gordon Pilley is a married travelling salesman specializing in women's underwear, who provided Juliet with garments in her size in exchange for sexual favors.

Miss Eulalia Hoppold, a globe-trotting female anthropologist with a deep interest in people is another suspect with no clear motive, and the Freel siblings round out the list of suspects. The Freels share a dwelling that is divided straight down the middle with tape, and the brother is expected to stay firmly on his half of their home, except for the weekly card game with the Colonel and Miss McLintock. Basil Freel is a former clergyman who claims to have lost his faith, although his sister's distaste for her brother stems from the fact that his defrocking came not from skepticism, but from his inappropriate interest in choirboys. Amy Freel is a far more jovial character, a woman who fancies herself an amateur detective after having read a great many mystery novels, and persistently nags Dover to be made an unofficial consultant on the case.

After interviewing all the suspects, Dover and MacGregor observe a few holes in some of their stories, and eventually realize which parties know far more than they are saying. A ransom note for Juliet leads to a fruitless stakeout outside a public restroom as a ransom demand is met but never collected. An angry accusation that Dover botched the ransom drop-off is quashed when forensic analysis proves that Juliet was dead after her fingerprint was placed on the note, as the minute sweat droplets that invariably appear in the fingerprints of the living are totally absent.

Dover jumps to a conclusion about the guilt of two suspects without much evidence, aside from MacGregor's realization that one suspect knows something that an innocent person could not have known. Convinced they are on the right track, Dover drags MacGregor along for a confrontation. Dover manages to get one party to confess through pure threats and bullying, leading to a skirmish and a grisly discovery as the hiding place of Juliet's body is revealed.

Dover has found his killers, but despite convincing proof of guilt, he lacks a solid motive. It is Amy Freel who comes closer to the truth of why the crime happened in the first place, as she writes up her theory of the crime in a letter to the police, naming two suspects, though she only gets one of the guilty parties right. She does, however, manage to deduce the correct motive, though both Dover and MacGregor condescendingly dismiss Amy Freel's theories as over-imaginative balderdash. Dover and MacGregor return to London, and though Dover's final words pooh-pooh Miss Freel's conclusion, it's implied that if the forensic team applies the same level of scrutiny to the guilty party's home as they did to the fake ransom note, the conclusions regarding the motive that Amy Freel deduced at the end of her unofficial investigation will be vindicated.

Assessment

One hesitates to call Porter's first novel her best, because that carries the unintended implication that all of her work is downhill from there. *D1* is certainly one of her best novels, though a few others may contend for the title of "best." It is an excellent introduction to the series, which neatly, concisely, and effectively defines the characters of Dover and MacGregor and their working relationship in a few short pages. The detectives, their personalities, and their highly dysfunctional approach to detection are fully formed, with the pair remaining essentially the same for the remainder of their adventures.

D1 embodies the template of all of the future Dover novels, with few exceptions. Dover and MacGregor are summoned to a small rural town to investigate a crime, deal with some sort of discomfort or inconvenience, the pair interview a series of colorful suspects, and eventually, the truth is revealed, sometimes by a stroke of inspiration on Dover's part (or less often MacGregor), and sometimes by a very fortunate twist of fate. Usually, the motive behind the crime contains some sort of dark twist, perhaps centering around some scandalous or otherwise taboo subject. People do sometimes commit crimes for money or love in the Dover novels, but the more memorable solutions show a killer striking to protect a shameful secret or protect some sort of perverse practice they enjoy.

Not all of the Dover novels can be fully solved strictly through logic–as the plot of *D1* illustrates, on occasion Porter crafts the narrative so the reader can figure out the identity of a killer by catching a slip of the tongue in a suspect's testimony, and then extrapolating the repercussions of that lie to get a better idea of who else might have been involved. But just as Dover and Miss Freel each only solved part of the mystery, it is possible to name the correct killer and never figure out the motive driving the murder.

The "whodunit" portion of *D1* is a fair play mystery. The observant reader can determine the identity of a killer through paying close attention to the dialogue, and realizing which suspect possesses knowledge that he or she should not have, which leads to the conclusion that the suspect who knows too much is the killer– or rather one of the killers. Once the identity of one guilty party is identified, it follows that someone connected to that person must also be involved in the crime. Other details about the mystery, such as how the "ransom" letter was mailed, can be figured out by listening to the seemingly irrelevant ramblings of innocent characters, and taking a logical leap as to how the killers adapted ordinary behavior to devious ends.

It's the "howdunit" that requires more than just observation and logic. In order to figure out the logistics behind the disposal of the body, the reader must do more than pay close attention and make reasoned deductions. The solution to Juliet Rugg's fate requires an imaginative leap—or perhaps a twisted mind—in order to determine. There are a few clues, including a seemingly innocuous quip by one of the villains, that presage the truth. Dover himself is frustrated by the absence of a body, and the paucity of leads. At one point, he ponders:

"As the chief inspector slipped gently towards sleep he brooded uneasily on the case as a whole. He didn't like these amateur jobs, he thought fretfully. Give him a good professional crime every time. All you had to do then was sit back and wait for some disgruntled villain or other to start singing. Then, when you knew which one of them it was, you just dolled up the evidence a bit and made it point in the right direction. Easy as falling off a tree. 'Strewth, he'd give his right arm for an informer on this case. It wasn't fair to expect him to go round searching for clues and making deductions and God knows what! He sighed deeply. Perhaps the body'd turn up tomorrow. Then they'd have something to go on… That's what he wanted. A nice solid body… dripping… with… clues… " (107-108).

A very skillful storytelling technique is the fact that the characterization of several suspects is often in doubt. Multiple suspects, when first interviewed by the detectives, take great pains to depict themselves in a certain way, defining their personalities and often boasting of their own flaws. These characters tend to paint their sins or shortcomings sympathetically or charmingly (at least in their own estimation), acting as if they are lovable or pitiable rogues. Then, a couple of pages later, another character dismisses the previous positive portraiture, suggesting that the braggadocio was based on lies. Even by the end of the book, the reader does not know the true nature of a few of the suspects for certain. Some might deserve to be in prison, or perhaps they are simply being slandered.

Porter uses grotesque characters to illustrate social ills and shortcomings in society. In *D1*, some of the characters are monsters, while others are lovely—albeit eccentric or even ridiculous—people. Porter had a knack for crafting literary miniatures—crafting distinctive, memorable characters in three to ten pages, allowing the reader to remember them as suspects, partly because their exaggerated flaws which reflect wider problems are so memorable. The elderly satyr who boasts of his sexual wantonness and delights in shocking his prudish daughter, the dissolute and drug-addicted refugee who narrates his tragic life story like a demonic joke, the uncaring and promiscuous mother of the victim, the would-be mistress of real estate who publicly mourns her failure to turn the profits she desires, the adulterous salesman, and the sad-sack defrocked clergyman who bewails—and likely lies about—his lost faith, all embody deadly sins. Most of the aforementioned characters are unpleasant or unsettling, but all are genuinely human, exemplifying vices in a grotesque manner while never falling into broad caricature. Readers see snapshots of severely flawed people, and the more perceptive may see cautionary tales as certain transgressions. The handful of likeable characters, like Colonel Bing, Miss McLintock, and Amy Freel, shine due to their ebullience of personality. They may be annoying to Dover, but they are far more congenial than their nasty neighbors, and they are friendly women who mean well. Characters like these three women temper Porter's generally negative assessment of her era, as she paints this time period as an era of mediocrity marred by a corrupt and ridiculous citizenry. Agatha Christie's legendary sleuth Miss Marple once remarked in the short story "The Tuesday Night Club" that "So many people seem to me not to be either bad or good, but simply, you know, very silly" (4). That sort of attitude runs throughout Porter's characterizations.

D1 exemplifies Porter's trademark—a darkly comic look at England between the early 1960s and 1980. During this time, England was still reeling socially, economically, and spiritually from World War Two, and the cultural upheavals of the 1960s were starting to reshape society. Porter's England is very different from the genteel country estates that are the stereotypical settings of Golden Age detective novels, a time usually defined as the period between the two World Wars, instead being a society of wealth, comfort, and safety, which makes the lethal violence seem all the more out of place and unsettling. Productions such as *Upstairs, Downstairs*, *Downton Abbey*, and *Gosford Park* all emphasize how England between the wars was a society with a strict class system, one where everybody knew their place, though the characters had very different levels of satisfaction with their roles in the English caste system.

The society Porter depicts in her novels is in a state of disarray, though whether England is falling apart or breaking free is a matter of interpretation. Many people are direction-less and isolated, the virtues of good behavior and Church morals are largely ignored and shunned, everyone is worried about money, even the wealthy, and the general impression of society is one of shabbiness and decay. Porter does not preach in her novels, but she presents a world that is at best crumbling around the edges and at worst falling apart at the seams. Though she never comes right out and denounces certain perceived problems affecting England, throughout the novels, there is a constant theme that there is a great deal of rot at the heart of contemporary society, and the root of the problems lies not in the flaws of institutions or economic systems, but in the souls of ordinary people. Porter does not push a specific agenda for improvement, though it is often hinted that traditional Judeo-Christian morality and a special concern for how one's actions may affect others might make major steps to improve the problems. Porter never looks back to the supposed "good old days" and there is no hint that society was better in the past. There are only constant assertions that society is severely flawed in the present and may get steadily worse if steps are not taken to fix the problems.

Moralizing may draw attention to social ills, but preachiness is rarely fun. Porter knew that she was writing a mystery novel that was meant to be entertaining. These are crime stories, not editorials. *D1* is Porter's opening salvo into her commentary on the unhealthy state of her society, but her focus was always on humorous detective fiction, rather than preachy message fiction. Retribution can come in different forms, and Porter ironically chose to craft her embodiment of Nemesis as the personification of vice.

Chapter Two: Dover Two (1965)

The Plot

D *2* opens with the detectives investigating the death of a woman who was killed twice. Isobel Slatcher was shot multiple times in the head and left for dead eight months earlier, and has been comatose in a hospital bed ever since. The doctors agreed that her odds of recovery were virtually nil, but someone was not taking any chances. Right after a newspaper article announced that she was on the verge of waking up, someone entered her room and smothered her with a pillow.

Dover, who is rumored to have a nasty habit of choosing a guilty party by taking a list of suspects and selecting who he will arrest by sticking a pin into the names at random, is convinced that the killer must be Isobel Slatcher's fiancé Pilot Officer Rex Purseglove. Violet Slatcher, the victim's older sister, is telling everyone who will listen that he is guilty, though Rex's laid-back father and overprotective mother are defensively proclaiming their son's innocence.

The investigation takes place in a particularly volatile situation, as the village of Curdley is torn by religious sectarian tension, with Catholics and Protestants in a constant state of friction ever since Henry VIII's schism from Rome. Nearly all of the local police officers are Catholic, and the Protestants believe that they're deliberately refusing to investigate the death of the Protestant Isobel Slatcher out of either spite or fear that a Catholic would be revealed as the killer. Meanwhile, the Catholics are tired of the constant barrages of accusations and slurs against them, and all of this frustration and resentment is constantly on the brink of boiling over into violence.

As outsiders, Dover and MacGregor find the townspeople of all religious persuasions slightly more amenable to talking to them, as they interview a domineering matron, cowed nurses, the local vicar, his housekeeper, a gang of Catholic toughs, a gossipy barmaid, a "freethinking" fish and chip shop owner, and the Chief Constable Colonel Muckle, who'd rather golf than work. Along the way, Dover recovers the gun used in the shooting through promises he cannot keep, and Dover's ego is constantly bruised by the saga of "Bigamous Bertie," a multiple murderer who wed many of his victims and has now been executed after a very public trial. Dover is deeply jealous of his successful colleague Detective Superintendent Percival Roderick, who is now a national hero for solving the "Bigamous Bertie" case and is frequently enraged by people asking him if he knows "Super Percy," who is now treated as a national hero. Dover hopes that a successful resolution to this case will lead to him getting a comparable measure of adulation.

The detectives spend most of the book acting under the supposition that both the shooting and the smothering were committed by the same person, but after following up on a scandalous rumor, Dover uncovers the identity of the

21

smotherer, and after an uncharacteristic burst of sympathy for someone involved in the case, plows through and finds out who shot Isobel Slatcher, albeit he only learns the truth while accusing an innocent person of the shooting, provoking a spontaneous confession from the real shooter. With both attacks solved, tensions in the village decline, and Dover departs with a surprising amount of respect from the local citizenry.

Assessment

All neophyte authors need time to find their natural style and develop their strengths, and it is common for authors to tinker with their tone and approach to their narratives early in their careers until they figure out what works best for them. Porter found her footing earlier than many others. Porter established the tone and narrative she would use to great effect for the rest of her writing career in her debut novel, but in her follow-up, she would experiment with darkening her light tone. The experiment, though aesthetically successful, was not repeated.

D2, particularly the second half, is the most somber book that Porter ever wrote. There are a few humorous lines to cut through the seriousness, but once the identity of the smotherer is revealed, the entire book is infused with sadness, as after that point the revelation of the truth comes across as a tragedy of love and despair rather than as a satisfying triumph of justice. Even Dover shows more emotion and empathy towards his fellow human beings than he does in all of the other nine novels combined.

The later chapters of *D2* are poignant and moving, but

they are not nearly as much fun or as diverting as the other novels. Seeing as how it was one of the first three books Porter wrote before being published, it illustrates how Porter was experimenting with her personal style and figuring out where her strengths lay and what her audience wanted. Wisely, Porter decided that her talents were best suited for a wry, often farcical style, and all of the subsequent novels in the series would be substantially lighter in tone than *D2*.

Just as Porter experimented with the tone of her novels, she also experimented with her characterization. Dover and MacGregor have no clear character arcs—the pair are essentially the same people in Porter's final novel *DBB* as they are in *D1*. In the later chapters of *D2*, we see Dover uncharacteristically caring about someone other than himself, and pursuing a case for reasons other than self-advancement. Nothing would ever stir a comparable level of emotion and selflessness in Dover again—he would remain a boorish antihero with no attachments to any other human beings, not any devotion to abstract concepts of justice, either.

Porter deepened MacGregor's character in *D2*, but in his case, the changes would stick. One particularly notable bit of characterization Porter inserts here is the fact that MacGregor is not always a sympathetic character. At the start of Chapter Seven, he's described as "a bit of a prig" (85). Indeed, through-out the later novels, MacGregor frequently annoys others with his superior airs and high opinion of himself. This prevents him from being portrayed as a sympathetic, long-suffering victim of the overbearing Dover. (The radio adaptations would soften MacGregor's character, portraying him as a victim of a rude and greedy boss who only once got a bit of his own back.) Porter's interpretation of MacGregor would indicate that to a certain extent MacGregor was responsible for his own troubles, meaning his perpetual link to Dover. MacGregor simply was not always likeable, and his ego earned him plenty of enemies at Scotland Yard. MacGregor became a victim of his own personality, as his superiors sought to punish his arrogance and presumption by pairing him with the Yard's most aggravating detective, and essentially locking the upwardly mobile young officer into career limbo.

While there are some well-crafted characters in *D2*, the collection of suspects is not quite so skillfully developed as the well-crafted miniatures in *D1*. Most of the characters fill their place in the plot well, but on the whole, the cast is much less memorable than in the preceding work. Violet, the victim's sister, filled with a thirst for vengeance, self-righteousness, and anti-Catholic bigotry, is the best-defined character of the main supporting cast, and the hospital's imperious matron is the novel's finest example of a memorable grotesque, but on the whole, most of the characters are rather ordinary, lacking the indelible freshness and satiric bite that would define Porter's best fictional creations.

Much more involving is Porter's satiric setting, as she depicts a society split in half along religious lines. Possibly inspired by "the troubles" in Northern Ireland, the town of Curdley is divided into warring camps of Catholics and Protestants. The religious strife subplot is at the heart of Porter's societal scrutiny. Notably, Porter does not attack actual religious belief or doctrine, and there is no push for ecumenicalism, nor does Porter push the common canard that religious disagreements are best solved by secularism. Indeed, the members of the community seem to have a vested interest in being divided into tribes, and the refusal to love one's neighbor is a matter that causes the villagers to define their own identities, as each half of the town is united by a strong dislike for the other half. There are no significant attempts for one half to convert the other, as there is no desire to assimilate the enemy camp. Everybody seems to be taking too much pleasure living in a permanent state of civil war, where the divisions that cleave the town into two actually strengthen the ties that bind both individual halves of the community.

The Catholic vs. Protestant friction is more of a class conflict than a theological divide. Indeed, the central clash is more about "yobs vs. snobs" than it is about transubstantiation vs. consubstantiation. The Protestant members of the community largely suffer from the sin of pride, believing in their innate superiority. The Catholics as a whole are less proper but also warmer. As a general rule in *D2*, the Protestants despise the Catholics because the Protestants believe that the Catholics are inferior to them, and the Catholics despise the Protestants because the Protestants believe that they are superior to the Catholics. In a parallel vein, the "freethinking" fish and chip-shop owner self-satisfiedly believes that his outsider status gives him a level of moral superiority as well. The schism is based primarily on cultural and class factors rather than on matters of faith.

Porter's stress on the tensions between the rival groups adds another important plot point: both halves of the town wish to see one of their enemies exposed as the guilty party. This is one of the rare occasions in a Dover novel where there is pressure from a person in power or an interest group to arrest a certain person (or person who fits a certain profile), *DGP* being the other example. Dover famously cares little about identifying the right person most of the time, preferring to make an arrest for the sake of closing the case quickly, though the evidence is usually so shaky that the wrongly accused is usually acquitted. (It is occasionally noted by Porter's omniscient narrator that the handful of successfully resolved cases that appear in published books are exceptions to the general rule.) What is easy to overlook is the fact that the guilt cannot be laid solely on Dover's shoulders. MacGregor can be given a partial pass due to his constant attempts to find the truth, and the fact that he cannot overrule his superior officer, yet the fact remains that MacGregor is simply not a consistently effective detective. Yet it is important to remember that higher-ups at Scotland Yard and prosecuting attorneys are also to blame, because they know Dover's reputation and refuse to scrutinize his work more closely, nor are there any passages depicting Dover's superior officers making a serious attempt to discipline Dover for arresting an innocent person, though there are occasional references to the fact that Dover has survived internal investigations for corruption or incompetence.

Dover's deep-seated loathing for MacGregor is not just personal, but professional as well, as outlined in this passage:

"Young detective sergeants were, in his considered opinion, the lowest form of police life, and he spent long hours complaining happily about their shortcomings and inadequacies. But, however scathing he might be about the present generation of young detectives, the last thing he wanted was to have a really bright one working for him. That would be murder! Detective sergeants should be seen rarely, and heard never at all. They should be humble and admiring witnesses of the brilliant feats of detection carried out by their superiors. Any contributions which they felt it incumbent on them to make should be proffered modestly and hesitantly. They shouldn't, thought Dover, twitching his nose crossly, discover something which, right out of the blue, might solve the whole bloody case. It put Dover in such a dilemma. If he followed up MacGregor's line of thought and it turned out, oh horror of horrors, to be right, it would be very difficult (though not impossible) to deny his sergeant at least a share in the glory. And on the rare occasions that Dover actually managed to bring one of his cases to a successful conclusion he liked the limelight to play exclusively on him.

On the other hand, if he refused to have anything to do with his sergeant's latest bright idea what, as MacGregor had so pertinently asked, the hell were they going to do next. It was all very annoying. Dover's underlip stuck out unhappily and he pushed his tea cup forward again for a refill. It really was very difficult. Still, he sighed pathetically, these things were sent to try us. With a bit of luck, he might still be able to pick MacGregor's brains while retaining the lion's share of the credit, if any, for himself. He had, after all, frequently done it before" (162-163).

Given Dover's abysmal track record for solving cases as a general rule, the fact that he manages to find the truth in *D2* shows that he can be a terrific detective if he can only overcome his deep-seated laziness. Of course, fictional mysteries depend on the ingenuity of the authors, and Porter shows her skill at leading her readers down the wrong path while always playing fair. A common trick for crime writers is to push one perspective or solution repeatedly, so the unwary reader accepts an erroneous false assumption about the case. The cleverest touch to the mystery stems from the possibility that the shooting and the smothering were committed by two separate people. For most of the novel, Dover and MacGregor assume that the same villain was behind both attacks. Repeatedly, as the pair go over their thoughts on the case, they postulate that the killer shot his victim, grew worried when he heard a report that she might regain consciousness, and then smothered her to assure her silence. The savvy reader knows that when a theory of the case is repeated over and over again early in the book, it is wise to view that narrative with suspicion. It is a clever approach, and by questioning it, the intelligent reader has a much better chance of solving the mystery by scrutinizing the suspects to find unstated but easily deduced motives. While the tone of *D2* is darker than most of Porter's other work, Porter's ingenuity and skill with plotting and clueing still shine brightly.

Chapter Three: Dover Three (1965)

The Plot

D3 does not start with a murder, but with a rash of poison-pen letters affecting the small village of Thornwich, an isolated hamlet that only survives due to the fact that it has a road running through it where shipping trucks speed through at dangerously rapid rates. Dover and MacGregor arrive on the scene, and though they feel like an anonymous person scribbling slanders is not the most effective use of their time, they investigate the case just as they would a mysterious death.

The townspeople include Arthur Tompkins, a friendly shop owner, and his wife; Charlie Chettle, an elderly man who enjoys hearing about Dover's work; a selection of barkeepers and domestic staff with varying levels of competence and hygiene; Mary Thickett, a supercilious companion and secretary; Miss Poppy Gullimore, a teacher with a reputation for civil disobedience; Dr. Hawnt, an elderly doctor who both publicizes and resents the fact that he's two-thirds senile; and Dame Alice, an imperious, condemnatory noblewoman who believes that she has the right and power to order about everybody in town. As Porter's omniscient narrator declares, "Dame Alice was an experienced committeewoman and never used one word if ten would do. She had found that one could bore one's colleagues into submission just as effectively as brow-beating them there" (62).

Early in the investigation, Miss Gullimore makes a weak suicide attempt by swallowing aspirins, and soon afterwards Mrs. Tompkins actually does die. Her death is ruled a suicide caused by gassing herself with her fireplace. After doing some digging, Dover and MacGregor conclude that Mrs. Tompkins' suicide was connected to her struggles with infertility, and the depression she felt after being thwarted in her attempts to adopt a black-market baby. The detectives cause some minor disruption in town after provoking the head of the baby-selling ring to run away, and they track down a woman who Mrs. Tompkins unsuccessfully tried to buy a baby from recently. Meanwhile, Dover's investigation and minor successes have made him a bit of a hero in town, and he luxuriates in having an audience buying him drinks and listening to his heavily embellished stories of his triumphs.

After a particularly awkward confrontation with a suspect that leaves Dover and MacGregor shaken to their cores, MacGregor observes something that leads Dover to take a deductive leap and claim that he has identified the author of the poison pen letters. While a horrified MacGregor hastens to point out to Dover that his deductions are shaky, Dover is convinced of the suspect's guilt, even though he knows he will never find enough evidence to make an arrest. Dover then devises an underhanded stratagem: he privately informs the local authorities that he is certain of his suspect's guilt. Lacking incontrovertible proof, the suspect will never face charges, but the rumors will spread and the suspect's social standing in the town will be forever destroyed.

Convinced that he has successfully solved the case even though there will be no formal conviction, Dover and MacGregor board the next train for London. At one point, MacGregor leaves Dover alone in the train car, and another character (not the one Dover accused of writing the letters) confronts Dover. Believing that Dover's presence on the train is no coincidence (it is actually a pure fluke of fate), the character spontaneously confesses to writing the poison pen letters, explaining that it was all part of a plan to kill Mrs. Tompkins and make it look like suicide. The killer explains how the anonymous letters were written, the suicide was faked, the motive, and reveals many other secrets, all the while being unaware that Dover has just accused an innocent person of being the anonymous letter author. After confessing fully, the true poison-pen author and killer throws open the door of the moving train, commits suicide with a handgun, and falls out into the night.

Once the door is closed, Dover resolves not to say a word about what just happened. He is quite content to let the village think the person he accused is truly guilty, and anyway, if he were to reveal the truth of what he just heard, his personal reputation would be damaged. Realizing that professionally speaking, the best course of action is to keep silent, Dover takes the path of least resistance, ensuring that the truth of the crimes will never be known.

Assessment

With the anomalously downbeat *D2* over, *D3* resumes Porter's distinctive comic, wryly satiric tone. There are none of the tears for the deceased that were shed in *D2*, none of the heartbroken determination to set things right that Dover so uncharacteristically displayed in the preceding novel. *D3* reverts to the series' permanent tone as a dark and witty romp, with frequent digs at types of people and certain segments of society in general. Most of Porter's Dover novels pick a specific target of English society for special scrutiny, and in *D3*, Porter's pen is used to upbraid those wealthy and prominent people who believe that by virtue of their wealth and social position, they have the right and the duty to control other people's lives and reshape their community in the manner that they deem best. Such attitudes are exemplified by the imperious, unpleasant character of Dame Alice.

Dame Alice is by far the most powerfully sketched figure in the book. Her title and economic status convince her that she is by right (if not law) the head of the town. Notably, Porter stresses that she is a petty tyrant of a very run-down town in Thornwich. Dover and the other residents often comment on what a dump of a village Thornwich is. The buildings are largely seedy and run-down, and multiple residents openly dream about moving to someplace more congenial, brighter, and less dirty. Thornwich mainly survives by being located on an extremely busy road that serves as a popular path for transportation, so travelling truckers often make stops and spend a bit of money in the area. In one of Porter's classic ironies, the road that is the lifeblood of the town is also its greatest danger, as the enormous trucks that go speeding down

CHAPTER THREE: DOVER THREE (1965)

the dark and busy path can easily strike an unwary pedestrian. As one publican notes early in the book, a man who crosses the road at night puts his life at risk (15).

Dame Alice shows no embarrassment over the state of her little fiefdom. A domineering figure who enjoys using her wealth and social position to control and humiliate those around her, she is formidable and unpleasant, and just the sort of person who gets under Dover's skin. Disliking her displays of power and her contemptuous attitude towards him, Dover despises her and seeks to give her the comeuppance he feels she so richly deserves.

Dover puts off meeting with Dame Alice for as long as possible, enjoying making her wait, but when the grande dame's demands coupled with MacGregor's pushing become too much for Dover to withstand, he comes to her home to discuss the case with her. Unfortunately for Dover, Dame Alice is much less interested in hearing his take on the case than she is in monologuing about her own theories on the anonymous letters and just which people with a perceived grudge against her might be trying to seek revenge through the venomous libels.

The meeting with Dame Alice is arguably the best-written scene in the book. Dame Alice continues to expound upon her own opinions at great length, blocking Dover from involving himself in the conversation or doing anything to make himself more comfortable:

" "Do you mind if I have a cigarette?" said Dover.

MacGregor, well trained, had the case half out of his pocket when Dame Alice's reply cracked across the room like a cat-o'-nine-tails in the hands of a sadistic master at arms.

"I certainly do mind! It is a filthy habit and I am surprised that a man of your standing and position should be a slave to it. It is nothing more than a breast substitute, you know. You can't have been weaned properly as a child."

Dover's jaw dropped in blank astonishment. Before he could rally, she was off again" (69).

Unable to get Dame Alice to slow down or allow him to get comfortable, Dover decides to employ "guerilla tactics used to confuse and lower morale" (70). He demands to use Dame Alice's lavatory, and manages to pierce her steely exterior by using the facilities for an extended period of time while making unsettling noises. This does not stop Dame Alice, but it does shake her.

By the end of this hours-long confrontation, Dover is desperate to arrest Dame Alice, simply to get a little of his own back in retaliation for her dismissive treatment of him. When Dover wrongly suspects Dame Alice of a minor crime, the incredible luck which has preserved his career thus far serves him well again, and he is spared the embarrassment of having to retract an actual false accusation, and even shamelessly turns the situation to his advantage, implying that he was aware of who the true guilty party was all the time. Later on, based on a twisted interpretation of an observation of MacGregor's, Dover wrongly believes Dame Alice to be guilty of a more serious crime. Knowing he has no evidence to back up his claims, Dover cleverly tells the local police his accusation over the phone and that while he's one hundred percent certain of the truth of his comments, there is insufficient evidence to take it to court. Dover is, therefore, able to poison Chief Constable Mulkerrin against Dame Alice, destroying her credibility amongst the local police. Dover is also aware that the telephone operator has a habit of listening in to conversations, and will probably spread the gossip to as many people as possible. The fact that Dover soon finds out that Dame Alice is completely innocent does not inspire him to take steps to wipe clean the stain that he has personally placed upon her name. The final scene of *Dover Three* makes it clear that Dover cares little for truth and justice compared to how he cares for his personal comfort, reputation, and coming out on top with his grudges.

This is therefore the first and only time we see Dover make an accusation out of sheer malice, with just barely enough evidence to justify the accusation. Throughout the series, we see Dover make correct accusations based on minimal proof, false accusations predicated on a genuine belief in the suspect's guilt, and attempts to pin the crime on a convenient suspect out of sheer laziness and a desire to wrap up the case, but while Dover on other occasions briefly considers arresting a suspect without cause simply because he finds that individual annoying, he is never shown actually arresting an innocent person, as his ire is usually dissipated or directed elsewhere soon afterwards, so the target of Dover's dislike rarely stays in the crosshairs for long. The point that most of Dover's cases are doomed to failure is repeated throughout the series, which indicates that either Dover is too lazy to habitually piece together a case against a random suspect, or that MacGregor has stepped in to prevent a palpably innocent person from being force-fed into the maw of the criminal justice system.

Over the course of this investigation, MacGregor does little to justify the high opinion he has of himself. Indeed, his vain assurance in his own abilities often seems to be rooted in little more than airy conceit, as he repeatedly misses the relevance of several clues throughout the course of the investigation. In one scene, MacGregor naïvely fails to realize that a woman he is interviewing is a prostitute, failing to see through her thick, possibly ersatz accent that she is not actually a French tutor. Dover feels no need to clarify the situation, and the reader may be amused at the fact that MacGregor is not nearly as worldly as he thinks he is.

The fact that neither Dover nor MacGregor distinguish themselves at solving this investigation should not let the reader off the hook. *D3* is actually one of Porter's simplest mysteries to solve, especially for a seasoned reader of mysteries. There are several potential suspects for writing the poison pen letters, although given Porter's heavy stress on the profile of the author as voiced by both Dover and Dame Alice, the savvy reader will quickly suspect that their suspicions are substantially less accurate than they believe. As the book progresses without an official murder, the intelligent solver of fictional crimes will take a close look at the unsuccessful suicide attempt, and the successful suicide, and after scrutinizing one of them more thoroughly, will get a shrewd idea of who is behind these mysterious goings-on, given the comparatively limited suspect pool.

The following comments are meant as an observation and are in no way meant as an accusation of plagiarism. Agatha Christie fans will note that there are many parallels between *D3* and Christie's novel *The Moving Finger*, featuring Miss Marple and published in the early 1940s, over two decades before *D3*. *The Moving Finger* also features a formerly placid English village turned upside-down by a series of anonymous poison pen letters which accuse the residents of all sorts of scandalous behavior. Early in *D3*, Dover's theories about the crime and his psychological insights as to why the author of such letters might engage in this behavior and send letters to oneself close mirror Miss Marple's comments in her summation explaining the crime. Furthermore, the *D3* plot point of a person allegedly committing suicide due to the contents of a letter, and the means by which the supposed suicide note is procured (a passage torn out of context from a larger letter) are directly mirrored in *The Moving Finger* (219). Given the originality of Porter's other work, and the fact that Christie's fame would make deliberate plagiarism easy to spot, and the countless other differences between the novels, the literary critic must proceed with some caution here. The parallels of the dialogue and suicide note's contents indicate that the similarities cannot be purely coincidental, but one cannot rule out the possibility that Porter read *The Moving Finger* at some point and unconsciously carried over bits of that book in her mind and incorporated them into her own work.

Though the mystery is among Porter's simplest, *D3* is an excellent example of Porter's early mastery of her comedic tone and provides a stellar characterization in Dame Alice, whose character arc shows how pride goeth before destruction, and a haughty spirit before a fall, especially when Dover has it out for such a prideful and haughty person.

Chapter Four: Dover and the Unkindest Cut of All (1967)

The Plot

The one major mystery that Joyce Porter left unexplained in her books is how DCI Dover and his wife have remained married for so long. Dover never exhibits any actual affection towards his spouse, and routinely comments on how marriage has completely evaporated any libidinous feelings he might once have possessed. In her rare appearances, Mrs. Dover exhibits either extraordinary patience, barely controlled temper, or elation at the prospect of widowhood. They have no children to keep them together, yet Mrs. Dover keeps cooking her husband enormous meals at home, putting up with his rotten disposition, and making few demands on her husband except in the short story "Dover Does Some Spadework."

As *DUCA* opens, the Dovers are going on vacation. Mrs. Dover, having a vast number of elderly relatives, frequently receives small legacies in their wills. Having recently been bequeathed several hundred pounds, Mrs. Dover has made two decisions. First, she will purchase a car; and second, she will learn how to drive. Dover is never comfortable in an automobile in the best of circumstances, as MacGregor, whose nerves have been permanently frayed from having to chauffeur Dover around, can attest. During the first few hours of their holiday, Dover has spent the lion's share of the journey berating his wife's motoring skills.

While Dover is dozing off, Mrs. Dover witnesses something shocking. A policeman bicycles towards a cliff, jumps off his bike, and then leaps into the sea. Dover is inclined to act as if nothing had happened, but Mrs. Dover insists that her husband investigate, and then report to the local authorities. The police are not that interested or respectful towards the Dovers until they realize that the suicidal police officer was possibly the Chief Constable's nephew. Once the Chief Constable decides to put Dover in charge of the investigation into his nephew's death, Dover's vacation is delayed, MacGregor is called back shortly before his flight to vacation in continental Europe, and Mrs. Dover is sent home.

At the police station, Dover witnesses an odd altercation. Two men are brought into the station for fighting, but as soon as a police officer suggests that they both be seen by a doctor for their injuries, one man freaks out and runs away, panicking at the mere mention of a doctor.

MacGregor arrives, and the detecting duo learn more about Wallerton, the small, quiet town where they are staying. Entertainment is limited, and any suggestions of moral turpitude are ruthlessly crushed. The upright nature of the town is rigidly enforced by the Ladies' League, an organization of the area's most influential women. They are known to have driven a shopkeeper out of business after he displayed inappropriate clothing in his window.

Despite not having a body, everybody is certain that Constable Cochran, the police officer who jumped off the cliff, is dead. The cliff has a reputation for being a popular suicide spot, and any person who falls in the water there is likely to be washed away into the sea, and the corpse will probably never be found.

Dover and MacGregor interview Cochran's landlady and learn that he behaved strangely right before his death. He cancelled a planned vacation and spent an entire week curled up in bed, after which he broke up with his longtime romantic interest. Before his "breakdown," as his landlady calls it, he had a reputation for being friendly with a shady figure in town. A local policeman tells them about another recent death, where William Hamilton, a local ne'er-do-well known for his womanizing, was found dead in his yard, horribly mutilated.

The investigation does not go well for Dover. An interview with the dead man's widow leads the irate policeman to get his foot smashed, which Dover has treated by a nearby female veterinarian. Uncharacteristically, Dover sends MacGregor away to focus on his own theories, while Dover takes tea with a local policeman and his wife, who is a prominent member of the Ladies' League. Dover learns that a lot of men with rakish reputations have each disappeared for a week, only to return with a changed personality. The man who Dover saw panicking at the police station recently vanished for a week. Another fellow, with a reputation for being a family man with nearly a dozen kids, disappeared for only a couple of days.

Dover and MacGregor interview an extremely nearsighted cab driver who drove Hamilton home the night he was killed, and realize that due to his myopia, the young cabbie might have been directed to the wrong place. Additionally, the cabbie previously had a reputation for being a peeping Tom, though after disappearing for a week, a prominent member of the Ladies League took him under her wing and got him a job as a cab driver during the night shift, when the streets are empty, and, in the Ladies League's opinion, anybody out that late at night deserves to be in a car accident.

The detectives discover that there is a hidden speakeasy in town, complete with flirtatious women and overpriced drinks. A low-level criminal Dover once arrested is in charge, and as they learn more about the seedy underbelly of Wallerton, they hear about the mysterious goings-on in town, including strange disappearances that are later chalked up to temporary amnesia. MacGregor becomes convinced that Hamilton became caught up in some criminal enterprise, and that these gangsters killed Hamilton, and that Cochran was on the take and killed himself out of fear that his misdeeds would be exposed and he'd be sent to prison. Dover has a very different theory that he chooses not to share with MacGregor.

Everybody who has read the title of the book can make a shrewd guess as to what is happening to some of the town's randiest men, and who is behind it. Dover certainly thinks he knows what is happening, and decides to set a trap with MacGregor as bait. He informs his hostess at tea that MacGregor has reputation for being a shameless womanizer, and soon afterwards, he sends MacGregor to visit the local veterinarian on his own. When Dover arrives, he enjoys himself as he delivers a gloriously hammy performance, informing his shocked audience that MacGregor is not supposed to be alone with women, as he has a habit of losing control, and then attacking and ravishing them.

41

Satisfied that the members of the Ladies' League believe that MacGregor is a pervert, Dover ostentatiously announces his departure, planning to return to rescue MacGregor and catch the parties behind the mysterious goings-on. However, Dover's attempts to return meet with unexpected difficulties, and a series of comic misadventure makes Dover doubt that he will be able to save MacGregor from a fate worse than death.

Dover's attempts to capture the parties behind the disappearances and the death of Hamilton fail, but MacGregor is unharmed, and the Chief Constable, furious at them both, expels them from the town. In the novel's final paragraph, it is implied that though the perpetrators are escaping justice, Dover's theories have been vindicated and that the Chief Constable has rejected Dover's conclusion to his own detriment.

Assessment

Though most of the titles of Dover novels are so generic that they could easily be interchanged without any decline in the appropriateness of the title to the book, *DUCA* is the only title to not only be appropriate for just one book but to be a spoiler as well. The cover of a recent paperback edition and a newly released ebook further underscores the nasty fate befalling the story's victims by prominently displaying a wicked-looking scalpel (Front covers). It does not require an exceptionally discerning or perceptive reader to figure out exactly what is going on in the coastal town of Wallerton. Indeed, having deduced what is causing the radically changed behavior in certain men, and having been introduced to certain stern and principled characters, it is not too hard to figure out who is behind the mysterious goings-on and what the motive is.

With the title being a massive giveaway, and the identity of the perpetrators being blatantly obvious, this is by far the easiest Dover novel of them all to solve. Yet despite the mystery itself being very clearly clued, this remains one of the best novels in the Dover series. The reason for that has nothing to with the actual mystery. The quality of the book is connected to the strength of the humor. *DUCA* features some of Dover's most outrageous moments, many of which stand in contrast to his standard acts of bad behavior. In most of his books, the comedy stems in part from Dover shirking his job from laziness and refusing to perform a proper investigation, or from bathroom humor connected to Dover's personal gastrointestinal idiosyncrasies. The uproarious final scene, featuring Dover's desperate attempts to return to the town, features the lethargic sleuth going to extraordinary lengths to complete his investigation and save MacGregor from a trap that Dover set himself. At no other point in the series is Dover so driven, though naturally, this determination does not last nearly as long as it should, as overexertion leads to him wondering why. Yet despite Dover leaning towards a return to inertia, he keeps on hurrying as fast as he can on his journey, all in an effort to save a man who annoys him and to reveal the truth behind the crimes. Truth rarely means much to Dover in his investigations, save for in the final act of *D2* where he developed an uncharacteristic emotional involvement to a certain individual involved in the case, and felt he owed the truth to that character.

While taking a brief time out from rushing to MacGregor's aid in order to partake in a sustaining snack, Dover starts to wonder if MacGregor is really worth saving:

43

"By the time he'd finished off all the remaining sandwiches and got through a couple of crumbly jam tarts, he felt much better. He was able to regard his predicament with a certain amount of detachment. It was damned hard luck on MacGregor, of course, but even for him, you could hardly call it the end of the world, could you? He'd learn to live with it in time. Lots of other people had. Dover sniggered to himself. Why, it might even turn out to be a blessing in disguise. The lad'd be able to concentrate on his job without dissipating his energies on a lot of external distractions. Dover chuckled." (155).

As usual, Dover's indolence dulls his sense of urgency.

Indeed, throughout the Dover saga, it's repeatedly illustrated how Dover has pretty effective detecting skills, but his intelligence is countered by his laziness. This characterization is reminiscent of Sir Arthur Conan Doyle's description of Sherlock Holmes's older brother Mycroft, who might have been a far superior sleuth to his famous sibling if only he hadn't been plagued by indolence. In the final pages of *DUCA*, the reader sees a glimpse of the man Dover might have been if he only cared. MacGregor and the local police are clueless, unable to use their creativity and lateral thinking skills to make the intuitive leap and figure out the motive behind the mysterious goings-on. Dover's performance is not perfect. His attempt to set a trap is most likely seen through by his intended quarry (or else his quarry was doing more reconnaissance before making a move and Dover tripped his snare too soon), and he fails to gather up that vital resource for closing a case—actual evidence. Of course, Dover does know where to find some proof that will validate the theories that the local constabulary denounce at the end of *DUCA*, but he decides not to interview the individuals who could provide the testimony and physical evidence that might lead to convictions, knowing that these victims have a deep-seated motive for not telling the world what happened to them.

In the midst of all the comedy are some very serious lessons. Certain criminal actions can only continue if the victims refuse to come forward out of fear or shame. In order to stop the crimes, a victim has to step forward and be willing to withstand the mockery or opprobrium of the general public. The issue involved is that certain crimes go unpunished because the living victim considers the fallout from the justice process to not be worth it, so silence and letting the perpetrator go free are considered the price of peace. This is a common issue for survivors of sexual assault, who consider a protracted criminal trial, along with the ordeal of testifying and being cross-examined by defense counsel, to be too much to bear, so many victims make a choice to avoid the stress of a courtroom confrontation and consider that letting their assailant walk free is an acceptable price to pay. The men targeted in *DUCA* face a similar situation. Each one of them has chosen silence or death as preferable to having their secret humiliation made known to the world.

DUCA features both Porter's most obvious mystery plot and some of her most sparkling wit and farce. The novel is not quite a battle of the sexes, because one side of the conflict is not aware that there's a war going on, and representatives of that side are in denial when the truth is pushed on them. The story explores what happens when social reformers take steps to fix what they believe to be the ills plaguing society, only to become more dangerous than the villains they seek to destroy. All of Porter's Dover and Hon Con novels critique and satirize the problems of contemporary British society, but noticeably

Porter never pushes solutions to these problems, other than suggesting that people ought to clean up their own houses first and attempt to identify their own personal shortcomings and improve them. Personal introspection is the best way to restore the individual, and individuals are the building blocks of society. Whoever would move the world ought to move himself first, and Porter argues that movements for social reform can degenerate into mob rule and vigilante injustice when righteousness blinds the activists to the consequences of their actions. Porter never tires of wagging her finger at the morally deficient in society, but *DUCA* is her clearest expression of her belief that often the supposed cures are worse than the social diseases.

Chapter Five: Dover Goes to Pott (1968)

The Plot

Dover and MacGregor are shipped off to the town of Pott Winckle, a quiet place where the main form of industry consists of the inexpensive lavatory products of Wibbley Ware Company Limited, specializing in clay items like chamber pots and toilet bowls. Daniel Wibbley the Third, the wealthy, arrogant, supercilious head of the company, is the unofficial ruler of the town due to his economic influence on the community. His daughter Cynthia has just been murdered—beaten to death with a poker—and Daniel Wibbley is insistent that his son-in-law John Perking is the culprit.

Cynthia disappointed her father by marrying a lower-middle-class travel agent at the age of eighteen. For the past three years, she has been living a quiet, simple existence as a housewife. Wibbley resolutely refused to provide his only child with financial assistance, although he freely admitted that the situation would change if his daughter provided him with a grandson. Alas, despite trying for three years, the young couple were not blessed with children. It is not until the investigation begins that the detective learns that the victim was pregnant.

Dover has been offered a comfortable position in the security division of Wibbley's company if he achieves the desired end of having Perking arrested, convicted, and sentenced to life in prison. The prospect of four thousand pounds a year gives Dover an incentive to investigate like never before, and Dover launches his investigation with only one suspect in his sights.* It is just as well that Dover believes that ninety-nine times out of a hundred, a wife is murdered by her husband. MacGregor is not so sure. All of the young Sergeant's instincts tell him that Perking did not kill his wife, and even though he is having trouble finding an alternative suspect, he is determined to spike Dover's guns to prevent him from railroading the newly widowed husband.

As the investigation progresses, Dover proves surprisingly sharp at puncturing MacGregor's alternative theories, as Dover observes telling clues that have completely slipped MacGregor's notice, such as the state of the television set and the contents of the kitchen garbage can. Even a neighbor's claim to have spotted a stranger visiting Cynthia shortly before her murder does not faze Dover, and he has Perking arrested over MacGregor's howls of protest. When Dover attempts to beat a confession out of his suspect, the third degree goes horribly awry, and it is Dover who winds up badly beaten.

After the coroner's inquest, Rosalind Wibbley, Daniel Wibbley's long-estranged wife, and his wife's cousin Ottilia get into a flaming row, as the women condemn the toilet magnate for his shabby treatment of the women in his life, and the long-estranged spouses tear into each other. Ottilia had no love for the victim, as when Cynthia married John Perkin, she essentially stole him away from her own cousin, Mildred. Mildred was passionately in love with John until Cynthia caught his eye. Meanwhile, the relatives Mr. and Mrs. Topping-Wibbley seem to take Daniel Wibbley's side, perhaps due to the fact that with Cynthia gone and leaving no heir, Mr. Wibbley is positioned to become the heir to the family business. The argument grows increasingly virulent, as Daniel attacks and sneers at his in-laws, and Ottilia denounces Cynthia as a selfish slut who ruined Mildred's life.

Daniel Wibbley is dead set against any aspersions being cast on his late daughter's name, and Dover realizes that any chance of that cushy job will be forever shattered if any embarrassing revelations are made public. Dover's hopes of a comfortable second career in the private sector take a heavy blow after he questions a pair of doctors, the first of whom informs him that John Perking is sterile and cannot possibly have fathered a child, and the second of whom confirms that Cynthia was overjoyed that she was finally pregnant, and could not wait to tell her husband he was about to become a father.

With MacGregor still doubting John's guilt and Dover insistent that the victim was no adulteress, the pair visit a medical laboratory, where due to a guilty party's histrionics, the truth behind the murder is revealed, a suicide is prevented, and Dover grudgingly abandons his hopes for a profitable new job.

Assessment

If solving a murder case "successfully" is defined as the fact that the detective has studied the evidence, identified the correct killer and motive, and made an arrest, then Dover never brings a case to an entirely successful conclusion. Every case is flawed in some way, such as Dover accusing the wrong person (and the true killer either confesses spontaneously or is unmasked by a confederate), MacGregor solves the case (usually thanks in part to Dover's inadvertent assistance), there is no evidence to arrest the killer, powerful forces save the killer from facing justice, or Dover gets the motive for the crime wrong. *DGP* is the closest Dover ever gets to a wholly successful closing of a case save for *D1*, where he got the motive wrong (In *DGP* he discovers the truth when a guilty party confesses rather than deduces it from clues he uncovered), though he does not solve the crime through drawing the correct conclusions from the evidence, but rather through competent following of leads and gathering evidence, which counts as solid police work, especially given Dover's notorious lack of energy.

Dover's unconventional enthusiasm is driven not out of sympathy for the victim, but out of a desire for a cushy gig in the private sector. The higher salary is an attraction for Dover, as is the possibility that he might be able to earn more money for very little work, though observing Dover's potential boss indicates that his future employer is not the sort of man to hand out a salary for doing nothing.

The best-developed character in *DGP* is Daniel Wibbley the Third, the cold, arrogant tycoon whose status as a captain of industry has left him in a position of great influence. In the opening pages, Porter writes, "Mr Wibbley wasn't exactly popular with the citizens of Pott Winckle but they certainly knew he was there. Either he paid their wages or he paid the wages of their customers. If his works closed down, the town would die. Pott Winckle knew this, and so did Daniel Wibbley" (8). Wibbley is a human iceberg with a cash register for a heart. He makes no secret of his loathing for his son-in-law, his disdain for what he sees as his daughter's poor choices, and his refusal to modify his views. He refused to attend his daughter's registry office marriage, and sent them the "popular model" of his company's complete bathroom suite, as "the deluxe one would have been a trifle pretentious" for their modest home in a housing estate (24). Wibbley even manages a nasty smile as he reflects upon his expression of disapproval—his comments to Dover make it clear that he's proud of himself for estranging himself from his only child after her marriage.

Wibbley expresses no shame or self-reproach in the way that he married his wife solely for her money, or how he discarded her when he was no longer dependent on her income and social connections. Nor is there the faintest flicker of self-reproach for his mercenary approach to business. Wibbley upbraids his long-estranged wife for not allowing him to divorce her at their daughter's funeral and publicly bemoans the fact that he was not allowed to remarry, provide Cynthia with a stepmother, and perhaps produce a male heir (125). Without making him into a cardboard villain, Porter crafts a portrait of a revolting quintessential narcissist with absolutely no insight into how his selfishness harms those around him. Wibbley luxuriates in the power he wields due to his wealth and status, but he is blind to the extent of his own nastiness.

DGP gives some insight into one of the few topics that can inspire Dover into loquaciousness, other than food, money, sleep, and his own health. When Wibbley declares that the abolition of capital punishment is "a most retrograde step," Dover concurs with a boisterous, "You're dead right there!… Disgusting, I call it! Well, it ties your hands, doesn't it? You can't scare the life out of some rotten little yobbo by waving life imprisonment at him, can you? And where's the incentive for us coppers, that's what I want to know? In the old days, you didn't mind taking a bit more trouble over a job if you knew the villain was going to get his neck stretched at the end of it. It gave you something to work for, if you see what I mean… I reckon they ought to bring the birch back, too… And the cat. Give 'em a taste of their own medicine, that's what I say. It's these kids, you know. They're the trouble. They're not brought up to have any respect for law and order these days. Why, you'd hardly credit it, but there's some of these vicious young devils that'd thump a copper as soon as they would their own mothers—and chiv him too, if they get half a chance. And why not? What happens to 'em if, by some miracle, we do nab 'em? They come up in front of some silly old beak who says it's all because they weren't potted properly when they were kids…" (19).

Wibbley is unimpressed by Dover's editorializing, as he prefers to hear the sound of his own voice, and is uninterested in anything other than seeing his son-in-law securely locked away from society.

No other Dover mystery has a prime suspect on the level of *DGP*. In most of the other mysteries (save the atypical *DCT*, which is not a classic "whodunit"), there are usually several strong possibilities for the role of killer. In *DCP*, in contrast, John Perking is the top suspect from the very beginning. Dover suspects him as soon as he learns he exists, based on the old—but surprisingly accurate—dictum amongst homicide investigators that when a married woman is killed, the husband is almost invariably behind the crime. This view is mirrored by Wibbley, who insists that his son-in-law is guilty and that the only formality is to gather up enough evidence to lead to a conviction and prevent an early parole release. The only person involved in the investigation to believe that they should be looking elsewhere is MacGregor, who suspects that the solution to the mystery is not as obvious as Dover and Wibbley insist.

MacGregor, therefore, becomes the surrogate for the arm-chair detective reading the novel, as the reader is bound to think instinctively that the solution to the mystery simply cannot be as easy as that, so there has to be another, less obvious solution to the crime. The veteran mystery reader will also anticipate a double bluff, expecting that if a suspect is so obvious that the reader will assume that he cannot really be the culprit, then the author is subverting the reader's expectations by making the most obvious suspect guilty after all. While maintaining this study's policy of avoiding the revelation of solutions unless absolutely necessary, it must be said that Porter manages to find a third way between these two solutions that still manages to provide a challenge for the reader.

Porter also provides an interesting touch by introducing and discarding a potential solution to the crime. Early on in the investigation, the detectives learn that Cynthia was visited by an unknown man, someone who MacGregor suspects could be the true killer. Porter breaks her normal storytelling style and introduces evidence through the means of an omniscient narrator, who reveals that not only was the visitor to the house a totally innocent person but also that MacGregor and Dover failed to find out the identity of the visitor (120-121). It is a notable and potentially controversial narrative choice on Porter's part, as she could have kept up the suspense of an alternate theory of a crime much longer. The truth about the visitor is revealed midway through the novel, long enough for the reader to reflect on the possibility that this stranger was the killer for a few chapters, but this fact could have been withheld until close to the end of the story just to keep the reader guessing and wondering longer. By timing the revelation as she did, Porter also manages to emphasize Dover and MacGregor's fallibility as detectives, for no matter how well they handle the investigation, they can still fail to reveal the entire truth of the case.

Despite jumping to a conclusion early on and allowing himself to be influenced by the victim's father in the hopes of a better job, Dover actually performs some of his finest police work in *DGP*. His knowledge of basic courtesy (despite his refusal to perform simple acts of etiquette himself), allows him to disprove one of MacGregor's theories, and his doggedness to track down evidence is unmatched in any other novel (70). Dover illustrates his observational and deductive skills by noticing perfectly good food in the garbage can and other discrepancies in the tidy kitchen (72). In the climactic scene, Dover also demonstrates a level of skill at extracting a confession in a friendly manner that ought to surprise longtime readers.

DGP is a well-crafted mystery that toys with the reader's expectations and assumptions while providing clever clueing for the reader to make a very shrewd guess at the events that led up to the murder.

* £4,000 in 1968 is the equivalent of £58,910.03 in 2019 after inflation. This is equal to $77,020.98 as of January 4, 2020. (https://www.inflationtool.com/british-pound?amount=400 0&year1=1968&year2=2019, https://www.xe.com/currencyc onverter/convert/?Amount=58%2C910.03&From=GBP&To =USD).

Chapter Six: Dover Strikes Again (1970)

The Plot

A massive earthquake has destroyed much of the small village of Sully Martin, and many people were killed. As the authorities were examining the wreckage, they found one body that clearly did not meet its end through the devastation wrought by the earthquake. Walter Chantry, who was visiting the damaged structures looking for injured people to rescue, was found strangled amongst the rubble. The local authorities decided to ask for the help of Scotland Yard, and instead of sending assistance, the Yard sent Dover.

Dover and MacGregor immediately notice that there's a lot about the crime that does not make sense. Why strangle the victim when bludgeoning could easily be passed off as injuries caused by the aftershocks from the earthquake? Why would the killer choose that moment to commit the murder? And who would have had a motive to slay a seemingly upstanding pillar of the community? As the investigation begins, Dover has no idea what the answers to those questions might be, and he is not motivated to find out, especially when he discovers that the hotel he will be staying at is unlicensed, meaning no alcohol can be sold there, and there is nowhere else in the damaged town where he can legally buy a drink. His pleas to have a goodly number of bottled spirits shipped to him (purely for medicinal purposes, he insists) are shot down by the local authorities, as they are barely getting enough food and medical supplies delivered to the remnants of the village as is. Without a constant infusion of liquor to keep Dover happy, it takes all of MacGregor's wiles to keep his superior from either selecting a suspect at random to arrest; or packing up, walking away, and writing the crime off as unsolvable.

The suspects include the victim's pregnant daughter and new son-in-law, who did not want the deceased to know their baby was conceived before the wedding; a cantankerous elderly woman with a fierce distaste towards Dover and his bathroom habits, a bubbly woman fascinated by the occult, a romantically-entangled trio of artists, a military man who is extremely protective of his mentally challenged teenage daughter, and a seemingly friendly hotel proprietor. None of them seem to have a really compelling motive for murder, and as is often the case with a Porter novel, the story is as much a whydunit as a whodunit, and the motive can only be gleaned by piecing together several scraps of conversations from throughout the book, identifying a contradiction in two of the suspects' statements, and then making an intuitive leap as to the motive for the crime based on this discrepancy and one suspect's unusual behavior.

In a rare occurrence in the series, Dover's life is actually in danger during this investigation. After a couple of days of questioning the surviving townspeople, an attack is made on Dover's life, when a string is attached to the top of the stairs, right by the door of Dover's second-floor room. The killer believed that Dover would rush out in the middle of one of his many nighttime calls of nature, stumble over the tripwire, and fall down the stairs to his doom. With a chill, Dover realizes he was saved by "a bit of providential constipation" (87). Dover's life was spared when a fellow guest, fed up with Dover's incessant noises during the night, crept up the stairwell seeking revenge, sprung the trap, and fell down the stairs to her death.

Dover is at his laziest here. Midway through the investigation, he refuses to leave his hotel room on numerous occasions, preferring to interrogate suspects or brainstorm with MacGregor from the comfort of his bed. Indeed, the climax of the book takes place in Dover's bedroom, when the Detective Chief Inspector, feeling particularly venomous towards MacGregor and wishing to deny him any chance at taking credit for the arrest, recruits the local policeman Superintendent Underbarrow to join him as he confronts his suspect with a lot of bluster and very little evidence. Remarkably, Dover's sharp accusations and surprisingly skillful wheedling break the guilty party down, but the ending of the book is perhaps the most downbeat of all of the Dover novels, with no humor—however dark—to soften the brutal blow, as the novel's final sentence explains how the killer left the world in a murder-suicide.

Assessment

This is another strong entry in the series, yet it never quite reaches the heights of the best entries. Part of this is due to the fact that the book, while still entertaining and humorous, does not have any deeply uproarious scenes on the level of Porter's finest comedic writing, such as the climactic scene in *DUCA*. Perhaps the most outrageous passage comes in the wake of Dover's first disastrous night at the local hotel, when one censorious guest loudly and disapprovingly calls out Dover in an indirect manner in front of everybody else at the dining hall, due to Dover disrupting all the other guests' sleep by clomping up and down the stairwell in his heavy boots and making the plumbing and cistern shake and clatter. The descriptions of the previous night's noisy events are cringe-inducingly funny. After this awkward lambasting, Dover wonders why he did not find a way to call out his accuser, and worries that he might be losing his grip (168).

The discerning reader will be able to solve the case by scrutinizing the suspects' testimony and finding a contradiction, just as Dover did. The motive, however, requires a leap of imagination and a particularly sordid idea as well, though watching the unusual behavior of the guilty party in one scene may allow the reader to put two and two together. It is all very tenuous though, and as the characters themselves say on multiple occasions, there is no proof. *DSA* is a fair play mystery—the reader has just as much to go on as Dover in order to solve the case—but cool logic alone will not lead to the correct answer—a dark and twisted imagination is also necessary to determine whodunit.

Additionally, it is never quite satisfactorily explained why the killer did not try to make the murder look like an accident. As both Dover and MacGregor note on multiple occasions, nothing would have been simpler than to hit the victim over the head with a bit of rubble, either killing him with one blow or leaving him face down in a muddy puddle to drown and expect the death to be written off as a tragic event caused by an aftershock or delayed damage to a structure. Strangling the victim only made the murder obvious. Similarly, the killer's attempt to kill Dover was quite clumsy, and the means by which the tripwire was affixed to the top of the stairs was so obvious that once again, murder would have been presumed immediately, rather than accident. These murders could have been passed off as accidents, but the killer's stupidity meant that the deaths would be ruled homicides.

One other bit of unfinished information comes from the fact that Porter never makes it precisely clear why the second victim was heading up the stairs to Dover's room. The reader is told that she was seeking vengeance against Dover for the disturbances he caused with his frequent nocturnal visits to the lavatory from a quick glimpse into her personal thought processes right before she died, but Porter's omniscient narrator does not make it clear exactly what sort of malicious plan she had in mind. In any case, Dover's remarkable luck held, and he was spared from the ill will of two foes.

One of the best-written passages comes from Dover's panicked suspicion that MacGregor might have been behind the attempt on his life. A word from the local superintendent gets Dover's imagination going, perhaps fueled by a touch of guilt for his behavior towards MacGregor over the years. Dover's genuine fear that the man closest to him may have finally snapped, coupled with his own cowardice at the thought of a homicidal person out to get him, shows Dover at his most vulnerable and funniest.

"Superintendent Underbarrow leaned back against the foot of the bed. "I must say I'd have thought we'd have done a bit better to start looking nearer home." Dover's heart missed a beat. Nearer home? God, why hadn't he thought of that before? He went cold as he thought of the risks he'd been running. Talk about nursing a viper in your bosom! Of all the ungrateful young bastards!…

He caught Superintendent Underbarrow by the lapels and gave him a good shake. "MacGregor! You've got to do something about MacGregor! It's your duty!"

"Well, now, and what would you like me to do, eh?'

"Strewth!" groaned Dover. He gritted his teeth. "I want you to arrest him, you silver-buttoned dummy! Damn it all, you've just said he was trying to kill me."

"I did?"

"All right, all right," said Dover in the hope that a bit of soft soaping might do the trick, "it was very clever of you. It never crossed my mind, I'll admit that. I knew he was a treacherous little brute but… The young bastard, I'll bet he's been planning this for years" (148-149).

Dover's sudden fear that his underling may have finally snapped is indicative of just how strained the pair's relationship is. Only Superintendent Underbarrow's observation that the person who tried to kill Dover was almost certainly Chantry's murderer as well quiets Dover's panicked fear of MacGregor, and Underbarrow writes Dover's frenzied ramblings off as a joke. Based on reading the earlier books in the series, a casual observer might suggest that the two might not get along, but that they work well together as a detection team. In *DSA*, Porter makes it clear that Dover and MacGregor are neither friends nor partners, and that not only is there no genuine trust or affection between the two, but Dover thinks MacGregor capable of seeking revenge for all his years of mistreatment, though such a thought leads Dover to only crippling fear and not penitence. Their partnership is one of inconvenience—Dover sponges off MacGregor and is annoyed by him; while MacGregor is impoverished by the constant scrounging, frustrated by his superior's indolence, and his career is tarnished by being linked with Dover. Given their overall low success rate (the unsolved cases are not recorded for posterity), the only people who routinely benefit from their partnership are the readers who are entertained by them.

Critical readers will find that *DSA* is a good entry in the series, but not a great one. Porter's skill for social satire is not as pronounced in this novel, as her barbs at certain types of people and the communities in which they live are rather minimal, due in part to the fact that this is a disaster area, and we actually see many of the members of the ruined village doing what they can to alleviate the situation, or at least making do with awkward conditions with minimal grumbling. An emergency has brought out the best in the village, and for the first time in a Porter novel, we see a community rather than a collection of different people who happen to live in the same area.

Simultaneously, the characterization is not as succinct and memorable as it is in her best work. In the finest Porter novels, a character may only have a few pages of presence, but they manage to make an indelible impression due to a skillfully chosen set of personality traits, with pithy dialogue thrown in to make the character memorable. The suspect list in *DSA* is not as colorful or over-the-top as many of the others in the series. There are no terrible egotistic aristocrats, no lovable eccentrics, and no figures where their character flaws have been stretched to become their defining hallmarks.

Instead, the *DSA* suspects are a pretty ordinary lot, filled with the sort of people one meets every day. The characters suffer from nerviness, pomposity, flightiness, hauteur, short temper, and other common negative traits, but the presentation of their shortcomings never rises to the level of grotesquery. That does not mean that they are boring or one-dimensional, but they are less memorable. None of the *DSA* suspects are on a par with *D1*'s Colonel Bing or *D3*'s Dame Alice in terms of lasting in the reader's mind long after the book is finished and replaced on the shelf.

While most of the settings of the Dover novels are pretty dismal places, the unpleasantness is usually the fault of those who live there, whether it's the Ladies' League in *DUCA* with their militant enforcement of morality or the unceasing religious feuding in *D2*. In *DSA*, the disruption and decay affecting the community are due entirely to a sudden natural disaster, rather than human iniquity or poor urban design. Unlike most of the other places Dover and MacGregor travel to over the course of their cases, Sully Martin gives the impression that it was a nice little area before the earthquake, and that it could be a pleasant place to live again someday, once the murderer is safely removed from the community and the town rebuilds.

One of the more disconcerting passes comes at the end, as the local superintendent makes no secret of his mild sympathy for the killer. This shows some of the attitudes of the time, where the actions that formed the motive for the crime were laughed off, dismissed, or even approved of in certain circles that thought themselves "progressive" and "enlightened." The ending of *DSA* is one of the rare instances where most contemporary readers are entirely on Dover's censorious side. The dark motive behind the murder adds to the downbeat ending, as the killer's insistence on exerting control even at the very end leads to tragedy. Most of the other Dover novels end with a wry joke. *DSA* leaves the reader slapped in the face with a flatly stated description of something horrific. This shocking finale could have been avoided if Dover had just been a little sharper and less anxious to relax. But then, if he had acted in such a manner, Dover would have been completely out of character.

Aside from the unusually heavy ending, *DSA* does not display Porter's literary strengths as strongly as many other novels, but it is still an entertaining entry to the series, and the solution demonstrates Dover's ability to pay close attention to detail even though he despises putting that level of effort into his job.

Chapter Seven: It's Murder with Dover (1973)

The Plot

The victim seemed like such a nice young man. Intelligent, amiable, and in his early twenties, Gary Marsh, a perfectly pleasant albeit somewhat dull fellow, seemed to have every reason to live. Of course, his background was a bit scandalous—everybody knew that he was born illegitimate and his father was unknown, and the villagers passed away many hours by theorizing about his parentage. Was the aunt who raised him really his mother? Was the father one of the military men who had stayed at the nearby camp? The odds-on favorite for the role of embarrassed papa was Lord Crouch, an impoverished aristocrat, though there's another group of gossips who contend that Lord Crouch's sister Lady Priscilla was Marsh's birth mother. But would this nobleman, who had lost so much over the decades, risk what he had left by beating Gary Marsh over the head?

Once again, Dover and MacGregor are summoned to a small village in order to investigate a murder. This is due to Lord

Crouch, who insists that the local police summon Scotland Yard right away. This annoys the local constabulary, who believe that Lord Crouch, who lives in genteel poverty in his enormous country estate Beltour with his sister, exercises a bit too much influence than he ought to in the community. At first, Dover is convinced that he's hit the jackpot in terms of accommodations, as Lord Crouch offers him room and board at his stately home, though the aristocrat's hospitality only goes so far. MacGregor is politely but firmly sent to stay at a nearby inn. Dover's anticipation to wallow in the lap of luxury is tempered by the fact that the siblings Lord and Lady Crouch live on a strict budget, with most of their home closed up except when it is being shown to the public for a much-needed influx of cash.

The brightest and funniest portions of the novel come from Dover's deep disappointment in the quality of his lodgings, particularly the food. Not only is Lady Priscilla a cook of modest talents, but she also prefers to cook vegetarian meals, a development that repulses Dover. Far from being the banquets Dover had hoped, the food he is presented mirrors the old joke about the unpleasant restaurant with two major shortcomings. The food is terrible, and the portions are much too small. Oblivious to her guest's enormous appetite, Lady Priscilla doles out minuscule portions of spinach soup and goat's cheese salad, with tiny bowls of jelly and cream for dessert, the last of which Dover unashamedly gulps down before his hostess can divide them into thirds. Furthermore, Dover proves himself to be a terrible guest, wreaking havoc with the plumbing, barking orders that he expects to be obeyed, and getting soused and asking rude questions.

The investigation follows the standard pattern for a Dover

book. Everybody connected to the case, from the aristocrats to the servants to the victim's aunt, is interviewed. The victim was engaged to the daughter of Lord Crouch's butler, and the bereaved girl seems more upset about no longer being set to marry at all than she is about the actual death of her fiancé. She seems aware that her options for matrimony are limited, and she takes a sudden and unwelcome interest in MacGregor, aided by her overbearing mother. There is a small-time hoodlum working for a bookie who needed to collect on a debt held by the deceased, as well as the proprietor of the local inn who runs a highly unhygienic establishment and might have lost his living if the victim hadn't been murdered and had been allowed to pursue his business dreams in a new motel management project. Other than the aristocratic siblings, the fiancée and her parents, and the victim's aunt, there are few other suspects, so the pool of possible killers is much smaller than most of the other Dover novels.

In this case, it is MacGregor who makes the big intellectual breakthrough in determining the killer and the elusive (but typically twisted) motive for the crime. Despite his innate reluctance to follow up on any of MacGregor's ideas, Dover pursues the theory and between them, the pair manage to make an arrest after a chance run-in with a witness shatters the killer's alibi. Though Dover usually does not derive much pleasure from his work, he manages to find the humor in his public revelation of the solution.

Assessment

Once again, the solution to the mystery cannot be determined simply by studying the clues. Just like in *D1*, *DUCA*, and *DSA*, the reader must make a creative intellectual leap in order to come up with the motive for the crime. While this is the first time in the series that MacGregor solves the lion's share of the case thanks to an inspired flash of insight, it should be noted that MacGregor has triumphed thanks to his succumbing to a habit that he despises in Dover: seizing onto a theory that just happened to pop into his head, and running with it despite no solid evidence to support it. MacGregor realizes the shaky foundation of his solution to the crime soon after recounting his narrative, but by that point, it's too late—Dover has latched onto it and chooses to pursue it.

Perhaps all the years of working with Dover has left its mark on MacGregor's detecting skills, because moments after coming up with a clever—and accurate—motive for the crime, and after inspiring Dover to accept the theory and pursue the suspect, MacGregor realizes to his horror that he does not have a single shred of proof to substantiate the charge. Unlike Dover, MacGregor still has a horror of arresting the wrong person, and also of the fallout that could affect his career if an accusation cannot be proven. When the duo cannot manage to convince the killer to confess, both men are willing to walk away from the whole affair. Dover abandons the case due to his characteristic sloth, and MacGregor steps away due to his reluctance to get caught up in the fray resulting from charges of false allegations, tempered by the fact that he believes that the killer may face justice outside the courts. It is only by pure chance that the investigators immediately stumble across a witness who can shatter the killer's alibi. This reflects the recurring theme in Porter's mysteries of the fallibility in the detectives. Logic and reason are not enough to reach the truth—inspiration, imagination, and creativity also play pivotal roles in unraveling mysteries, and there's no guarantee of finding sufficient evidence to lead to a conviction. Porter always stresses the role of chance when it comes to investigations, for a killer can either be too clever or too lucky to leave behind enough clues to lead to an arrest, and a chance mistake or the fateful presence of a witness can completely change a culprit's fate.

In *IMD*, Porter focuses most of her social satire on the characters of Lord and Lady Crouch, the titled aristocracy living in an enormous home yet scrimping by in extremely straitened circumstances. Notably, Lady Priscilla knows that in the current socio-political climate, her social position is not what it once was. A glimpse into her mind tells the reader, "Whatever other shortcomings she may have had, Lady Priscilla knew her place. And in this modern, egalitarian society it was right at the bottom of the pecking order" (105). Lady Priscilla has absorbed the changing social mores and realizes the precariousness of her own place in society, and worries about upsetting Dover. Though she initially takes umbrage to his blunt accusations, she swiftly develops a feeling that after all, she deserves this questioning. She does not command power, and despite one temporary burst of temper, her general demeanor towards Dover is one of deference, both out of concern for his work as a policeman, and also out of a desire to be a proper hostess. It should be noted that Porter makes a point of Lady Priscilla's high breeding, as she witnesses Dover's gluttony and atrocious manners at the table, and falls back upon her training as an aristocrat to make no sign whatsoever that she is aware of the piggish behavior that has taken place in front of her (18).

In contrast, her brother, Lord Crouch, may lack the wealth to really control the village, but he still acts as if he commands authority, such as when he tactfully but firmly informs the local constabulary that he really must insist on having Scotland Yard called in to investigate the crime. As Porter allows the reader to see into the thoughts of the representative of the local police force, it is clear that the officer in question finds Lord Crouch an annoyance, but due to considerations of the aristocrat's social position and power to influence certain figures and committees, the proper deference must be paid. It should be noted that one representative of Scotland Yard, having once visited Lord Crouch's estate with his children and paid twenty-five pence apiece for the privilege of doing so, considers he was ripped off and is bitter about it (2). Outside of his own little fiefdom, Lord Crouch commands no respect or fear from the police, and Dover's presence is sent as a rebuke to the nobleman for his presumption.

Lord Crouch is probably unaware of how little esteem he earns outside of his hometown, for he acts as if the title he wields bestows authority upon him. He consistently plays the part of benevolent leader of the community, and he is constantly focusing on preserving an aura of dignity. For example, Lord Crouch is six foot seven inches tall, and he makes a point of refusing to stand next to people shorter than he is, on the grounds that it makes them both look ridiculous (3). He is seemingly unaware of the ridiculousness of his own situation, as his gigantic home is a white elephant he can barely afford to keep. He admits to Dover that his father's death duties led him to sell off most of the family antiques and the contents of the wine cellar. As Dover's frequent gastrointestinal distress leads him to discover, the conditions of the lavatory are none too solid. The staff of servants has been reduced to the bare minimum, and Lady Priscilla cooks her own meals with an eye on cheapness over quantity. The only stream of income that keeps everything together is the money paid by the tourists to explore the house. Though the point is never brought up, having no recognized legitimate heirs and minimal income, the future of his estate is in some doubt after his death. With the death duties arising from Lord Crouch's eventual demise, barring some unexpected reversal of economic fortune, it seems probable that Lord Crouch will be the last of the family line to actually hold title to the house and land.

Porter entertainingly emphasizes the difference between Dover and MacGregor's reactions to the economic troubles of the nobility. Dover could not care less about the titles and supposed glamour of the aristocracy, but he does like the idea of living it up in a cushy mansion, with plenty of free food and lodgings, and the odd valuable antique or trinket that he might be able to slip into his pockets unobserved. When he learns that their relative poverty makes it impossible to provide him with the five-star accommodations and amenities he desires, Dover's temper is the stuff of legend. Dover fails to make the slightest effort to be on his best behavior as a guest in Beltour House.

In contrast, MacGregor, not coming from a wealthy back-ground himself, but having gone to a posh school and fancying himself an up-and-comer, is totally sympathetic to the aristo-crats of limited means. He practically tears up when he sees the way they are forced to economize, and mourns how few servants they have (10). The theme of sympathy for the upper classes is carried on to great comic effect in the Hon Con novels, where the aristocratic detective frequently mourns her limited means and constantly economizes, despite having inherited an annual income that is the envy of most of the village.

The aristocratic siblings are the best-developed suspects by far, but the next-best crafted suspect, who is fully, gloriously, and humorously developed in a single short scene is Miss Milly Marsh, the victim's aunt. In a brief conversation with Dover and MacGregor, she is revealed as a cold, condemnatory, and judgmental woman, who exerted complete control over her nephew's life, including his paycheck. Porter does a superb job of capturing the essence of the woman's character through brief lines of dialogue. When asked what sort of person her nephew was, Miss Marsh humorlessly replies that he was "a miserable sinner... like the rest of us" (57). Furthermore, she blames her nephew for being born out of wedlock and finds his getting murdered unbearably scandalous, saying he brought "shame on my name both coming into this world and going out of it" (56). Given the influence his aunt held over his life, it is not surprising that Gary Marsh sought escape in a most likely loveless marriage.

The depiction of Marsh's fiancée and in-laws is cleverly drawn. There is no attempt on anyone's part to assert that this was a case of true love. His fiancée Charmain Tiffin is desperate for a husband—any husband. Porter quips that whatever Marsh's reasons for choosing to marry her were, it was unlikely to be because of physical attraction. Porter's omniscient narrator informs the reader that Charmain "was actually twenty-nine, claimed to be twenty-six and looked a good forty" (88). His prospective father-in-law, Arthur Tiffin, Lord Crouch's butler, is an imposing figure at work, but a much more laid-back figure at home. His wife divides her attention between her domestic tasks and her determination to get her daughter married off, and in a couple of tart tongue-lashings, makes it clear that she blames her spouse for frightening off the previous potential sons-in-law. Mr. Tiffin's protestations that one boyfriend was already married and another had a predilection for little boys have no effect on Mrs. Tiffin. For her, Charmain's single status is all Mr. Tiffin's fault. Out of pure malice, Dover suggests to Mrs. Tiffin that MacGregor might make a suitable mate for Charmain, leading to some extremely awkward moments.

The relationship between Dover and MacGregor is as strained as ever in this entry. Dover initially takes great pleasure in taking up residence at the manor house while MacGregor is shipped off to bunk at the humble village inn, but Dover's smugness turns to fury once he realizes that MacGregor's meals are far more satisfying than his own. Dover also implies on two occasions that MacGregor may be gay, once in a fit of high temper to his hosts as he complains about his assistant, and once when he and MacGregor discuss the sexuality of one character, and Dover snidely tells MacGregor "it takes one to spot one" (134). Given the insight into MacGregor's mind as he gazes at an attractive receptionist at one point in the novel, as well as similar scenes throughout the series, Porter emphasizes that Dover is simply taking a shot at his underling and that MacGregor's interests lie entirely in women.

Ultimately, *IMD* is a strong entry in a series with no genuinely weak books, marked mostly by its satiric glimpse at a peer's family in decline, and by the humor produced by Dover's trademark boorishness. Though the mystery itself requires more inspiration than logic for the reader to solve, it continues Porter's career-long theme of illustrating how private vices can lead to destruction for innocent people.

Chapter Eight: Dover and the Claret Tappers (1976)

The Plot

DCT opens with a sharp break from Porter's standard formula. Here, Dover and MacGregor are not called to some remote village in the countryside in order to investigate a crime. Dover is right in the center of the action from the very beginning, for he is kidnapped as he is leaving Scotland Yard one evening.

The general reaction amongst his peers is restrained jubilation. MacGregor can hardly believe his luck, and the long-suffering Mrs. Dover is thrilled to begin a new life as a widow. Of course, Dover is not dead yet, but as the authorities refuse to pay the cash ransom and release the two prisoners the kidnappers demand to be set free, everybody figures that it is hard luck on Dover, but they cannot negotiate with criminals, so there's nothing for it but to leave Dover to his fate.

Surprise and disappointment are in the air when Dover is released—alive, well, trussed up in a giant plastic bag, and dumped on the street. MacGregor cannot hide his heartbreak, and Mrs. Dover decides that her plans to start her merry widowhood with a little holiday should not be spoiled by an inconvenient little detail such as her husband being alive. Dover is called upon to investigate his own kidnapping, and he and MacGregor realize that his afternoon tea was doped in order to make him stay asleep until late that evening when it would be easier to abduct him in a nondescript taxicab.

The detectives act on the theory that the abductors are politically motivated radicals, probably politically militant students. The kidnappers dubbed themselves "The Claret Tappers," a reference to a slang term for punching somebody in the nose to make it bleed. A couple of scenes are described through the gang's perspective, and it is revealed that there are three men and one woman involved, and some seem much more hesitant to engage in violence than others.

Upon investigating the two prisoners the Claret Tappers wanted to be released, it becomes clear that the pair were not jailed for political reasons. The first is an amicable, nonviolent multiple bigamist, and the second is a shoplifter who protests her innocence and lasciviously hits on MacGregor. An attempt to track down the woman who doped Dover's tea through tracing her blue suede jacket proves similarly fruitless.

Eventually, the house where Dover was held captive is found, though Dover is surprisingly hesitant to provide any details about his place of capture. As it turns out, he was kept in a small, windowless bathroom, and despite his traditional lack of shame about using the aforementioned room, he believes that it would be too embarrassing for him to take if the location of where he was held became public knowledge. His attempts to keep this point quiet are foiled when the forensic scientist at the scene discovers a huge quantity of dandruff on the floor of the bathroom that could only have come from Dover.

As the reader is informed multiple times in the novel, most of Dover's investigations end in abject failure, and Dover's inquiry into his own kidnapping initially falls into that category. Months pass, but then the Claret Tappers strike again, kidnapping the grandson of the Prime Minister and killing the baby's nanny in the process.

Dover and MacGregor are recruited for the task force, despite Dover's desperation to sleep. The pair are drawn further into the case when the Claret Tappers demand that Dover deliver the ransom himself. Whining every step of the way, Dover miserably trudges up a steep incline in an isolated area and finds a little Shetland pony and a note telling him to stuff the money in the saddlebags. The pony trots off and disappears, and so do any hopes of catching the Claret Tappers.

Time passes, the officer in charge of the task force is trying to figure out how to pin all the blame for the failure on Dover, and tensions are high until MacGregor sees some of Dover's scribbles, and draws a clever conclusion. MacGregor wrongly thinks that Dover has come to the solution first, and Dover, unwilling to admit he's stumped, allows MacGregor to think that he's solved the case, but arranges a meeting with the task force so MacGregor is allowed to enjoy a few moments of glory and explain his theory, while Dover subtly laps up the lion's share of the credit.

The narrative jumps over the last legs of the investigation, and flashes forward to a few days later when the Claret Tappers have been rounded up and the Prime Minister's grandson has been safely recovered. Dover missed out on the climax of the case due to a chronic attack of diarrhea, and he is forced to pump MacGregor for the details on how the happy and satisfying resolution was achieved, despite his resentment at asking his subordinate for answers to unsolved questions about the crime. Most galling of all, Dover is denied the honors and reward he feels he deserves for helping to recover the boy and vents his frustration by declaring "There's no bloody justice!" (203).

Assessment

Porter shakes up her standard pattern dramatically in *DCT*. With the murder occurring late in the book and no doubt as to who committed it, the focus is on the kidnapping and the Claret Tappers' mysterious motives. With Dover as the kidnapping victim, it gives the normally disinterested detective a deeper motive to figure out who is behind it all, but even Dover's thirst for vengeance is tempered by his innate laziness as the case progresses.

DCT provides some brief glimpses into Dover's life and psyche that are not explored anywhere else in the series. In those few instances where the reader has been shown glimpses of Dover's home life, Mrs. Dover is portrayed as resigned to her husband's unpleasantness and fits of temper, but who often puts her foot down to get her own way, such as when learning to drive or when finding out who's been poking around her garden shed. Some of the more sentimental readers might be excused for theorizing that beneath all of the grumbling and tantrums that there must be some level of fondness between the Dovers. Perhaps not a buried passion, as Dover's occasional assertions that life with his wife has killed all carnal appetites will attest, but still, a certain level of affection. Porter quashes any such romanticism, presenting Mrs. Dover in a state of restrained jubilation after her husband is judged unlikely to return home, and being so delighted at the prospect of moving in with her sister, that even the fact that she is not actually widowed can stop her from adopting her dream lifestyle for her golden years, albeit only temporarily (25). There is a brief moment that might be poignant for anybody else but Dover, as the detective grumbles with a touch of hurt feelings, wondering if his wife was even the least bit worried about him or if there was some little part of her that truly wanted him to come home unharmed, muttering, "You'd think she'd be glad to have me back!" (108). No further comment is given, but there is a real sense that Dover does not have a single person who cares for him in the world, due in part to his own fault for being such a repulsive bully.

Dover certainly cannot count any of his co-workers as friends. Another deviation from the standard pattern is the fact that there is no fictional village riddled with flaws, but Porter does direct her satiric eye towards Scotland Yard. In Porter's eye, Britain's police force is not staffed with selfless civil servants so much as it is with self-interested bureaucrats motivated by petty grudges. The delight his bosses feel at possibly finally being rid of him is open and unabashed. Dover has long been a carbuncle to Scotland Yard, a widely loathed and distrusted figure who nobody wants in their department, but who has found a place in Homicide and cannot be dislodged from it. With the additional insight into Dover's superiors, the reader learns just how often the powers that be have tried to catch Dover in the act of an offense that could get him fired, only to be thwarted by a combination of Dover's incredible luck and his innate skill for self-preservation (11).

The barely disguised satisfaction resulting from Scotland Yard announcing it will not pay a ransom for Dover illustrates that the thin blue line does not protect the force's laziest member.

The theory that MacGregor might possess some deeply buried affection for his boss is also shot full of holes, as MacGregor exhibits more happiness during his brief freedom from Dover than he ever shows during the rest of the series combined. MacGregor briefly luxuriates in the possibility of a brighter work life and a resumed upwards trajectory for his career, and even contemplates making the ultimate show of joy—buying a new hat for Dover's funeral (29). The reader may briefly sympathize with MacGregor after seeing his spirit crushed by Dover's return, but Porter hastens to show that MacGregor's being chained to Dover and the consequent career limbo is not just due to chance. *IMD* revealed that MacGregor believed that his lack of promotions was due to his name being forever linked with Dover in his superiors' imaginations, but in *DCT*, it is shown how MacGregor's pompous, cleverer-than-thou attitude and his obvious high regard for himself has hurt his career, as evidenced by the disdain his superior officers show him during a climactic scene where the young detective fails to hide his belief in his own brilliance. At one point, MacGregor's tone leads his superior Commander Brockhurst to "wonder if he hadn't been a bit hard on Dover all these years" (149).

If Dover realizes the extent to which his personality has alienated him from the rest of the world, he makes no effort to change in order to earn the affection he currently lacks. Indeed, many of the wittiest portions of the book come from his trying to maintain his dignity in the wake of the kidnapping, whether by portraying himself as braver than he was or by his frantic attempts to prevent the rest of the force from realizing that he was kept locked up in a lavatory, a fact that Dover fears will make him the target of ridicule. If Dover had any real insight into his behavior, he would realize that nothing his peers could learn about his confinement could make them respect him any less. Dover's penchant for using violence to get suspects to talk is on full display, and Porter reveals that he has no trace of chivalry in him, when the omniscient narrator declares, "Dover had no scruples about hitting women, indeed on the whole he preferred it. There was less danger of retaliation" (64).

DCT is also unique in that it provides a glimpse into the workings of the gang, showing a couple of meetings where one member convinces the others of the wisdom of releasing Dover alive and unharmed. The gang members' brief conversations show them to be a bit crude and a little dangerous, but they are not hardened criminals and they never appear to show genuine malice for anybody (25-28).

The tone of the investigation is also radically different from other installments in the series because the reader knows that most of the people Dover and MacGregor interview are innocent. In other books, most of the interviewees are potential murderers, and the reader knows to treat them as suspects. But in *DCT*, the people who are questioned are nearly all clearly blameless witnesses (or at least are prisoners convicted of nonviolent offences), who are connected to the investigation by pure happenstance. There are no breakout characters, and none of the supporting cast is sufficiently developed or humorous enough to stand out, as in Porter's best characterizations.

DCT is not so much a "whodunit" as a "cat and mouse" story, as the narrative focuses upon catching the members of the gang. There is no twist that reveals that the anonymous members of the gang are individuals introduced by their real names at any point in the novel. The main mystery that the reader has a fair chance of solving is a "whydunit." Why are the Claret Tappers making such odd demands? Why are they calling for the release of prisoners that seemingly have no connection to them? And what is the relevance of their supposed political manifesto? The answers to those questions are critical to the eventual capture of the criminals, where MacGregor pieces together some stray, undeveloped thoughts of Dover's and figures out how to track down their quarry.

As usual, Porter fills the novel with humorous quips and Dover's comically bad behavior, but the novel's funniest moment is arguably the climactic scene where a highly reluctant Dover is forced to deliver the ransom money. Dover throws the carefully calculated plans into disarray when he points out that he does not drive, smashes his walkie-talkie in a fit of pique, and his horrendously out-of-shape condition means that it takes him far longer than expected to climb a hill to convey the ransom cash, especially when he finds the two bags too heavy to carry, so he takes them one at a time, setting down one and doubling back to pick up the other, leading Dover's police compatriots to go out of their minds with frustration.

Radically different in tone and style from any of her other Dover novels, *DCT* is a refreshing break from the usual pattern, which also provides insights into just how low Dover and MacGregor are held in the esteem of their superiors.

Chapter Nine: Dead Easy for Dover (1978)

The Plot

As is often the case, this Dover novel opens with a couple of police officers in a small village discussing a murder, and realizing that they had better call in Scotland Yard for assistance. Scotland Yard, ever resentful to oblige, does just barely enough to constitute helping, and spitefully sends along Dover to investigate, with MacGregor in tow, in order to solve the death by bludgeoning of an unidentified young woman.

At the beginning of the investigation, Dover is characteristically enthused about solving the case. This is not due to a newfound passion for justice, but because Dover has discovered that there is a well-paying security job in the private sector that he believes he would be perfect for, and with visions of his new salary coupled with his early retirement pension dancing happily in his head, Dover decides that he needs to bring this case to a rapid and successful close in order to assure his getting hired for this lucrative position. Of course, in Dover's estimation, a "successful" close doesn't necessarily mean finding the true killer, just crafting a sufficiently solid case to make an arrest that will hold long enough for him to become comfortably ensconced in his new job before the defendant is released.

The usual collection of colorful suspects greet Dover and MacGregor. The corpse was found hidden in the bushes by the gate of a recently deceased wealthy man, who was looked after by his niece and sole heiress Miss Charlotte Henty-Harris. Dover, more concerned with making an arrest than finding out the truth, immediately cottons to the theory that Miss Henty-Harris killed both her uncle (despite not one atom of proof that the rich old man died anything other than a purely natural death) and the anonymous girl, which predictably produces an indignant uproar from Miss Henty-Harris.

The other suspects include Mrs. Esmond Gough, a rabble-rousing feminist who wants to become the first female bishop ordained in the Church of England, and her mousy husband, the Brigadier, who does not share his wife's passions but enjoys the comfortable income she earns through donations to her cause. Other suspects include Clifford de la Poche, a flamboyant man who preys on choirboys; Mrs. Yarrow, his housekeeper, who once lost a job after coming after a bossy employer with the fire-irons; Mr. and Mrs. Raymond Talbot, a pompous banker and his wife who are involved in the occult; and the Bones family, who are blessed with some rambunctious children and no discipline, one of whom uses Dover's famous filthy bowler hat as a chamber pot.

Bodily functions play another pivotal role in the plot when Dover is stuck in a public convenience that has not been stocked with paper. After being compelled to use the only bit of paper in his pockets—the application form for the job he is seeking—the loss of the form symbolically causes Dover to lose interest in leaving the force. Reasoning that he has got a fairly good thing going at Scotland Yard and that his job security might not be as secure at a private company, Dover decides to maintain his career status quo and loses interest in a quick arrest midway through the investigation.

Yet with MacGregor's prodding, the search for the killer continues. The autopsy reveals a few clues. The victim was in the early stages of pregnancy, and a paper bag used to repair a hole in one well-worn shoe was from a restaurant some distance away. Dover reluctantly goes on a road trip with MacGregor, as the trail leads from the restaurant (where the dead girl was a waitress), to her former school, to the victim's adoptive parents, to a charity for unwed mothers, and finally, to the home of one of the decedent's distant biological relatives, where Dover discovers a clue that leads him to the solution, though he refuses to share what he's found with MacGregor until he returns to the village to confront the killer face-to-face.

In a twist, the person Dover accuses makes a full and unprompted confession, but the party Dover thought was responsible was only an accessory, while a second party performed the actual murder, and the person confessing has no idea that accessories meet the same legal fate as the people who actually perform the crime. As the story ends, Dover smugly basks in the triumph of a successful conclusion, and MacGregor regretfully resigns himself to the fact that with Dover not taking early retirement, the two of them will be stuck together for some time to come.

Assessment

DED reuses the plot point from *DGP* where Dover is stirred from his lethargy thanks to being offered the metaphorical carrot of a far more lucrative job in the private sector. Dover likes money and hates having to travel across the country to stay in generally uncomfortable accommodations, but he despises the effort that comes with actually having to work for a living. Despite the fact the MacGregor practically has to drag Dover across the country for interviews, Dover manages to do some of his best investigative work, despite his desire to arrest everybody who annoys him, a list of people that grows longer with each passing chapter.

There is one investigative thread that remains dangling. When it is revealed that the victim was pregnant, the detectives naturally wonder if the father of her unborn baby (or potentially someone close to the father who may have had a problem with the kid on the way) was involved. This is a reasonable avenue of inquiry, as up onto that point, there is no other solid motive for murdering a girl in her late teens. As the narrative progresses, the reader may suspect that the man who impregnated the victim will be unmasked at the climax. But the revelation of the baby's paternity never occurs. The identity of the father of the second life lost is never revealed, and ultimately, his identity is irrelevant to the crime.

Porter focuses much more scrutiny on the behavior and hypocrisy of the dead girl's adoptive parents. In the brief scene where Dover and MacGregor interview the couple, shortly after identifying the victim, the parents are portrayed in a highly unsympathetic manner. They are not shown as being cruel or abusive, but they are depicted as materialistic, self-absorbed, and incapable of recognizing their own shortcomings. When interviewed, their primary reaction is not grief, but rather indignant resentment. The victim's mother views her late adopted daughter as a failed investment rather than as a lost loved one. Mrs. Wallace is filled with vexation over the fact that they spent a considerable amount of money raising a child who wound up getting murdered on them when they could have spent that cash on vacations, a car, and other luxuries (117-120). A further irony arises from the fact that the Wallaces cut off all ties with their family and moved away when they adopted Pearl. Ostensibly, the pair claim this is because they did not want anybody to reveal to Pearl that she was not their biological daughter, but given the characters of the pair, it is certainly possible that there could have been other reasons for severing all connections with their old lives. In any case, Mr. Wallace claims that Pearl cooled towards her parents once she learned about her adoption, though once again this claim must be taken with some skepticism. Given the uncaring personalities of the pairs, it certainly does not strain credulity to suggest that the rift started much earlier, and the revelation of the adoption serves as simply a convenient excuse on Mr. and Mrs. Wallace's part to bowdlerize their relationship with their adopted daughter.

In terms of characterization, the suspects and other minor characters in *DED* illustrate Porter's skill for crafting a memorable figure in just a few pages. The most memorable is arguably Mrs. Esmond Gough, the activist calling for women's ordination in the Church of England. Porter is very subtle in illustrating her flaws, but what's conspicuous by its absence in her loquacious outpourings is any serious mention of God, faith, the supernatural, or any of the ethics connected to religion. She only seeks a position of power and prominence, where she can receive respect and engage her flair for the dramatic. Her enthusiasm lies in activism and making impassioned speeches to crowds. Her crusading is centered entirely around satisfying her own ego, rather than serving the Lord.

Miss Henty-Harris, the niece of the recently deceased wealthy man, is a more subtle character, as the less attractive aspects of her nature are hidden at first, but easily uncovered through some not particularly rigorous questioning. Her early comments portray herself as a long-suffering yet devoted caretaker, though as the interview progresses, she grows increasingly defensive, stressing how much she believes she deserves her inheritance, and her refusal to share it with her other family members, who in her opinion did nothing to earn a penny of their wealthy relative's money. Miss Henty-Harris presents herself as a lamb, but underneath the fleecy exterior is a woman who may or may not be a wolf, but who is far pricklier than she originally appears.

Porter turns her social criticisms to the educational system in her portrayal of the harried Headmaster of Mottrell Comprehensive School (the ineffectual, cowardly man is not provided with any proper name), who clearly has no gift for educating or inspiring young people. Like in the Hon Con story *RCSC*, Porter seems to deplore the breakdown of discipline and virtue amongst the nation's teenagers, as the school has devolved into a war zone, and the headmaster has barricaded himself up into a well-protected fortress of an office, with only his fear of his own students for company. He fears a physical assault by a violent student and lives in terror of "Pupil Power" (115). Similarly, the Bones family has no control over their unruly children, who are allowed to run wild, and the parents can only apologize and clean up their progeny's messes. In a more serious vein, the police force is unable to protect children from a sexual predator in Clifford de la Poche, whose preying on vulnerable boys is well known, but the police are unable to make a case (one would hope that they would be able to find at least one of his victims willing to testify against him, but apparently he bribes the boys he preys upon), though there is a throwaway line about keeping an eye on him in the future until they can finally be sure of a conviction (135).

In *DED*, the crime is solved not by clever leaping to the correct conclusion based on a smattering of clues, as Dover often does, but through dogged, determined detective work. Dover and MacGregor perform interviews, and the one piece of physical evidence that proves useful, the paper bag used to patch a hole in a shoe, is analyzed thoroughly and the clues are followed up competently. For a Dover investigation, the threads of an investigation are followed diligently, and all of the clues and potential avenues of exploration are examined to their fullest extent. Dover's discovery of the truth is due in part to his amazing luck, as he wanders onto the critical clue by accident as MacGregor is interviewing a witness. MacGregor would have uncovered the important clue himself given only a little more time, but Dover found it first and took pleasure in torturing his subordinate by refusing to share his information until the last possible second.

The intelligent and perceptive reader has a fair shot at figuring out the culprit, so long as the armchair sleuth does not fall into the trap of accepting the motives that Porter provides, and instead considers additional possible reasons why someone might wish a pregnant teenager dead. The cleverest clueing comes from Porter demonstrating the sort of lies that certain suspects tell, and by figuring out what they might be trying to hide, one can make a very shrewd guess as to what dark secret one of the suspects might be trying to hide.

DED is a very good mystery, and it shows Dover at both his best and his worst. We see his skill as a detective, along with his usual flaws and his frequent digs against women who get pregnant out of wedlock. While Porter's skill was not flagging in the waning years of her mystery-writing career, the novel is permeated with a sense of disappointment and even despair over the state of society. The more one learns about the victim's personality, the less sympathetic she is, as she comes to embody youthful self-obsession, fueled by resentment towards the transgressions (both actual and merely perceived) of her elders. There is a sly dig at the power of the labor movement, as Dover's attempt to bully one young waitress is nonchalantly waved aside, as she notes that her father, a highly placed union official, would happily start a strike to avenge any attack on his daughter. She declares, "My dad's a shop steward!... You try pushing me around, copper, and you'll have a general strike on your hands!" (103).

Overall, the world Porter depicts is an increasingly tawdry one, where the people in positions of authority prove horribly inadequate to the tasks at hand, save for the extremely competent head of an adoption agency. There's no sense that catching the person who murdered Pearl Wallace will lead to everything being set magically right, but Dover's solving of the case does create the sense that without really meaning to, he has made a notoriously messed-up world a little bit better.

Chapter Ten: Dover Beats the Band (1980)

The Plot

I n the final Dover novel, Dover investigates a homegrown gang of neo-fascists and achieves the seemingly impossible: career advancement.

The story opens with a dead body being found in a garbage dump in Muncaster. The head has been mutilated beyond recognition, but there are a couple of tiny clues in the victim's stomach that prove critical. The first is a small blue bead known as "funny money," a currency used in lieu of real cash at a chain of disreputable holiday retreats, which means that vacationers are compelled to buy drinks and snacks without really understanding how much they're overpaying for their treats. The second clue is venison, the victim's last meal.

After Dover manages to browbeat Sir Egbert Rankin, the grotesquely mercenary and boorish owner of the dilapidated holiday camp Rankin's Holiday Ranch at Bowerville-by-the-sea into spilling information as to which of his camps used that particular shape and color of "funny money," the detectives head to a shabby campsite, watched over by the caretaker,

Captain Maguire. Maguire plies Dover with plenty of drinks, assuring that Dover never suspects him of any wrongdoing. The investigation is made much easier by the fact that venison was only served one weekend, and that the only group likely to contain the dead man during that slow period was the Dockwra Society, a group of stamp enthusiasts.

Dover and MacGregor start tracking down the members of the Dockwra Society, including a shady doctor and an animal-raising lady with an anti-Semitic streak. All their suspects are clearly hiding something, but they're unsure what it is until they visit Mr. Osmond, another Dockwra member, and Elvira, a young officer assisting them with the case, recognizes the suspect as an undercover police officer.

Furious at having his cover exposed (even if it is only to other police officers), Osmond forces Dover, MacGregor, and Elvira into a car and takes them to Sven, his handler at Special Branch. Sven reveals that the Dockwra Society is not really about stamp collecting, but instead is a front for a fascist organization that seeks to take over the country and persecute groups it dislikes.

Osmond tells the story about the night the victim was killed, explaining how he infiltrated the group after much trouble, and when the head of the organization announced that there was a traitor in its midst, he thought that the Dockwra Society's leader was referring to him but instead was talking about the victim, known as Mr. Knapper. Knapper, who was an agent working for Israel tasked with infiltrating the group, was caught and then given a "trial" at the campsite, and was swiftly found guilty. A deck of cards was divided amongst the attendees. Whoever got the Knave of Clubs was expected to execute the prisoner, and the person holding the King of Spades was compelled to dispose of the body and mutilate it to prevent identification, though steps were taken to make sure nobody could witness who did what.

After finishing the story, Special Branch tells Dover that Osmond had nothing to do with the crime and that Dover should let the matter rest so as not to imperil Osmond's undercover work. Normally, Dover would jump at the chance to stop working, but Special Branch's condescending attitude chafes him, and he decides to dip his toe into office politics, since one of his superiors, Commander Punchard, is a mortal enemy of the head of Special Branch, and would love to show up Special Branch if possible. After a fiery meeting leads to a green light to continue the investigation, Dover and MacGregor interview the remaining members of the Dockwra Society, all of whom stick to the same story centering around a flat-out denial of any legal wrongdoing. Despite their best efforts, the detectives are unable to break anybody and fail to glean any more useful information.

Dover and MacGregor retreat to their office, feeling as if they have hit a brick wall with their investigation. As they reflect upon the scanty evidence, a stray comment by MacGregor ignites Dover's imagination, and Dover immediately extrapolates this minor bit of evidence into a logical explanation as to who must have committed the murder and disposed of the body. MacGregor is stunned but mostly convinced, though he hurriedly reminds Dover that they do not have any solid proof. A little thing like incontrovertible evidence never stopped Dover before, and he immediately rushes off to Commander Punchard to share his theory.

Punchard decides to play his cards for personal gain rather than spite, and after Special Branch is informed of the killer's identity, special steps are taken in order to prevent a scandal.

93

The murderer gets off scot-free aside from being forced to emigrate, Punchard gets a cushy new job and a title, and our antihero Dover is not left out in the cold. He is finally given the promotion to detective superintendent he's desired for some time.

Assessment

Dover's last full-length adventure is an important one, politically and socially. As Dover is battling the threat of fascism and domestic terrorism in England, the stakes are a little higher than many of his other cases, which focus on more or less private murders with no political ramifications. This case, featuring a malevolent and reasonably well-organized gang of malcontents who wish to overthrow the government and install a white supremacist regime, has considerably higher stakes than any of the other cases with the possible exception of *DCT*.

As the novel unfolds, it is illustrated that the Steel Band does not pose a genuine threat to Britain's political structure. The organization's aims are certainly nasty, but their numbers are small, and they lack the military and political clout to actually overthrow the government, and given the extreme nature of their views and limited financial funds, it is unlikely that they could even manage to win an election for a single parliamentary seat. Of course, subversive political groups are watched because they have the potential to grow and spread like cancers, and commit individual acts of violence. As Porter illustrates, sometimes radical groups can gain victories by subverting the integrity of the system they seek to usurp and overthrow.

The closing pages of *DBB* illustrate Porter's criticism of a specific type of government corruption: the determination to avoid scandal at all costs. The true perpetrator of the crime is shielded from consequences because the public revelations of what was done in the name of law, order, and the existing British political system, would cause an uproar, possibly leading to the discrediting of powerful people or even entire institutions. Better to hush up the whole affair and let justice remain undone, because the consequences would be just too dire, or at least embarrassing to the people in charge of the nation.

Porter is not the first crime author to explore the consequences of what might happen if the leaders and institutions that are supposed to protect the people and their way of life are revealed to be whited sepulchers. Sir Arthur Conan Doyle's Sherlock Holmes and Agatha Christie's Hercule Poirot took on multiple cases to hide government incompetence or criminality for the greater good of the nation, though both great detectives made a point of declining to cover up serious crimes and refused to serve as the toadies of corrupt political figures, and both Holmes and Poirot were willing to let scandals rock the foundations of the nation's establishment if it meant getting justice for innocent victims. G.K. Chesterton's collection of short stories *The Man Who Knew Too Much* is one of the most famous crime books to address the idea of the government having a vested interest in covering up the truth when a person in a place of influence is caught committing a serious act of wrongdoing. Each story is told by a government insider, who explains to a journalist how a powerful person committed a crime and why it was necessary to keep the truth from public knowledge. At the end of the book, the journalist voices the reader's indignation that justice has been left undone for so long, and it is implied that all of the hidden secrets will be released to the public. The titular character admits that great wrong has been done but defends his nation as being worth defending, despite the corruption that haunts it (230-233).

In a traditional mystery, a criminal disrupts the social system by breaking the law, and the apparatus of the state goes into action to restore order. In stories like the ones described here, the situation is flipped somewhat, as the influentially placed criminal's lawbreaking imperils the state's reputation and authority, and the apparatus of the state acts to protect itself, placing the avoidance of scandal over the pursuit of justice.

Based on the light yet unsettling tone in which the cover-up is described, Porter's personal moral compass is aligned with Doyle, Christie, and Chesterton, but her central characters are not. Dover expresses no moral qualms about the cover-up, as long as he gets his metaphorical piece of the pie. Notably, the reader never learns what MacGregor thinks of the whole situation, and there is no hint that MacGregor has received the slightest morsel of compensation in exchange for his silence. Nor, for that matter, is there any indication that MacGregor will leak the truth. MacGregor's reaction to the whole situation is a mystery that will never be solved.

While most of the earlier novels focused on satirizing the personal foibles of individuals and social follies of small and isolated communities, *DBB* takes aim at the establishment of England, focusing on the effectiveness with which it handles domestic threats, and also the skill that insulates it from scandal. As the denouement to the novel indicates, the authorities would rather let a killer go free than let their public image get a black eye. Porter's omniscient narrator explains that a cover-up has been put in place to save Special Branch from embarrassment or public scrutiny, writing that "the great British public were thus enabled to retain their faith untarnished in the police, the Secret Service, the Monarchy, parliamentary government and anything else that took their fancy" (168).

As a mystery, *DBB* relies upon the clever interpretation of clues. By identifying a certain action which was *not* taken, and pondering the means by which the crime was committed, the reader can develop a reasonably shrewd idea of what happened the night of the crime and can identify the killer not long after that person first appears in the novel. Once again, the solution requires an intuitive leap based on the provided information of the crime, and the cleverest readers are likely to piece together the clues that point in the direction of the perpetrator long before Dover, especially when all but one of the suspects share a crucial characteristic that proves to be a vital clue. For the experienced solver of fictional puzzles, this is one of the easier fair play Dover mysteries, though the book is no less entertaining due to this fact.

The one prominent shortcoming of *DBB* is the characterizations of the suspects and supporting cast. There are no breakout characters, no humorous new grotesques that embody certain sins and shortcomings, only a handful of unpleasant suspects and a few members of the police force are introduced, and there is no literary magical trick to make them appear larger than life. Even the perpetrator, though better drawn than nearly all of the other suspects, is not especially memorable or colorful, nor does the perpetrator embody a certain set of character flaws that cause that person to serve as a satiric indictment of how a human being can go very wrong.

In contrast, after a little under two decades of investigation, Dover and MacGregor are still wholly themselves. MacGregor is Investigator Eager, throwing himself confidently into the case, following up clues, and using all of his strength to propel Dover forward in the investigation. Meanwhile, Dover is still wallowing in his personal vices, generating humorous situations through his continued gluttony and laziness. The pair actually work well together, as MacGregor's dedicated enthusiasm continues to offset Dover's sluggishness, and Dover possesses the ability to look beyond the obvious and piece together the truth through leaps of logic even when MacGregor cannot go beyond a certain point in his reasoning.

Dover is often on his worst behavior over the course of this case, whether he's carousing himself into near-oblivion at the summer cottages, acting as if he is trying to set a world record for how many calories he can eat, or even bucking the orders of the higher-ups out of sheer bloody-mindedness and resentment at being told what to do. Dover's triumphant apotheosis to the rank of detective superintendent is a bribe rather than an accomplishment, but this point means naught to the sluggish detective.

In the middle of the book, Porter's omniscient narrator pays tribute to Dover's cockroach-like ability to endure and thrive on the job:

"Although Dover was a right bastard, he was a lucky one. He was a survivor. They might call him Scotland Yard's most unwanted man. They might complain that he made their posh new headquarters off Victoria Street look untidy. They might claim he had trouble remembering his own name and that he wouldn't recognize a clue if it jumped and bit him. They might even assert that the usual method of picking out the murderer was by means of a pin, but what they couldn't deny was that Dover was still there. Hundreds of far better men had fallen by the wayside while he plodded shamefully on—determined to draw his pension or bust. Dover had been bloody-minded from the cradle and he was buggered if he was going to change now" (110-111).

Dover's ultimate promotion is the one nod Porter gives to this being the last in the series. Unlike other fictional detectives in their final books, there is no poignant death scene, no retirement, no threat to his position, and no major life upheaval, only a step up the ladder and the promise of more investigations in the future. Dover and MacGregor both end the series as essentially the same men they were at the beginning, remaining almost entirely unchanged from the way they were when they first started digging for the truth in *D1*.

Chapter Eleven: Dover: The Collected Short Stories (1995)

P ublished five years after Porter's death, this anthology of the Dover short stories provides a look at Dover and MacGregor's partnership in a much more condensed format. With a few exceptions, the stories follow the same template as the novels—the pair are called to investigate a murder, suspects are interviewed, and after a bit of reflection, the guilty party is revealed, usually involving a twist or unexpected motive. The stories were first published in *Ellery Queen's Mystery Magazine.* The volume features an introductory essay by the critic and mystery writer Robert Barnard, and a postscript by Porter's brother, Reverend Canon J.R. Porter.

The Stories

Dover Pulls a Rabbit (1969)

Dover's day off is interrupted by the bludgeoning of a woman in her own home. The scene of the crime is some distance away, and the journey is complicated by the fact that Dover has consumed a concoction of senna pods in the hopes that the laxative will soothe his sensitive digestive system. The trip to the crime scene is complicated by Dover needing to make frequent stops, and Dover makes his way to the bathroom the moment they reach the house that the victim shared with a housemate, a fact that will later prove quite useful in solving the case.

Despite constantly forgetting the victim's name and calling her "Miss Rabbit" instead of her real name, Miss Ebbitt, Dover manages to impress the local constabulary—and astound MacGregor—by identifying the killer within moments of meeting that person, all thanks to some keen observation and a few clever extrapolations from stray remarks.

Dover Tangles with High Finance (1975)

Dover and MacGregor are called to the offices of a prominent soap and detergent company, a corporation that "gives back to the community" by buying works of art and antiquities so they are not sold overseas. The valuable objects are then put on display, earning positive public relations for the company, and turning a profit as the treasures gain value. A leading member of the company's board of directors has died after drinking a glass of poisoned sherry at a meeting, and the other four members of the board are suspects.

True to character, Dover is less interested in the murder than in the boxes containing the pricey possessions of the victim and suspects, including cigarette cases, lighters, a fountain pen, and other items made out of precious metals, along with luxurious leather wallets stuffed with cash. MacGregor has his hands full trying to keep Dover's grubby paws from filching souvenirs though he cannot stop his superior officer from palming a high-end cigarette and running someone else's comb through his greasy black hair.

The suspects include a supercilious aristocrat, an impoverished titled figure who supplements his income by stealing office supplies, a blustering military man, and a Central European scientist with a flair for the dramatic. Each points the finger of suspicion in the direction of the others, but it is Dover who once again shocks MacGregor who solves the case through his examination of the suspects' possessions.

Dover and the Dark Lady (1972)

A man is found dead from a gunshot wound, and it looks like a suicide, but Dover and MacGregor are compelled to dig deeper to identify what really happened. The man was divorced, and his ex-wife was supposed to come visit him right before he died, but she claims that she never kept her appointment. Is she lying? If not, then who is the mysterious woman who has been seen around his flat? What sort of relationship did she have with the victim? As the investigation progresses, the detectives uncover a great deal of rancor between the divorced spouses, and a small circle of individuals with secrets they desperately want to keep hidden.

In the end, it is MacGregor who pieces together exactly what happened, but only after an embarrassing admission by one of the suspects. Despite this qualification to his subordinate's triumph, Dover is not pleased.

Dover Does Some Spadework (1977)

This unique tale is the only Dover story where the pair are compelled to take on an unofficial investigation. Mrs. Dover starts the morning by serving her ungrateful husband a massive English fry-up breakfast, only to be rebuked for an absence of kidneys on the platter. In retaliation, she demands that her husband look into a break-in at their garden shed. Nothing was stolen, but one item in the incredibly tidy shed was disturbed: a single spade was placed backwards on the shed wall. Mrs. Dover wants her husband to use his day off to find out who picked the lock and borrowed her spade without her permission. When Dover balks, she threatens to stop cooking for him.

A sulking Dover decides that if his wife is going to force him to work, then misery loves company, and a nonplussed MacGregor is called to Dover's home to assist his boss. MacGregor points out that a surreptitiously borrowed spade is likely to have been used to bury something. Dover's mind turns to stolen valuables, while MacGregor wonders if it might have been used to bury a body. In the tradition of Harry Kemelman's classic short story "The Nine Mile Walk," Dover and MacGregor take the limited clues at their disposal and extrapolate them into a detailed theory of a covered-up crime based on inferences and reasonable deductions. Just as the pair are planning to make an arrest, MacGregor turns up a bit of testimony that turns both men's conclusions upside-down and backwards.

Dover Goes to School (1977)

In this story, Dover and MacGregor investigate a strangling at an adult education center. The victim was lobbying against these special weekend classes, claiming that they were a wasteful drain on public resources. This gave the visiting lecturer on icons and the school staff a motive for murder, and the other suspects include a collection of lecture attendees, including the victim's much younger girlfriend, who came late, well after the victim had already started hitting on a married woman.

In a twist, Dover jumps to a conclusion and identifies the killer despite MacGregor's misgivings, although Dover's theory about the means of murder is swiftly refuted by the eager-to-confess killer. The closing scene shows MacGregor showing a surprising outreach of friendship to a killer, putting old school ties over decorum.

Dover Without Perks (1978)

The one thing that Dover really enjoys about investigating cases are the little perks he gets when investigating suspects. Most of the time, the people he interviews, acting out of a feeling of obligation to be hospitable, ply him with tea, cakes, treats, and, if he's lucky, alcoholic beverages and cigarettes. If MacGregor is not around to stop him, sometimes Dover manages to pocket a valuable household trinket as well. There is no hard-and-fast connection between economic status and generosity. Sometimes aristocrats are parsimonious and the middle-class bestow a massive bounty upon their guests, sometimes the reverse is the case.

In "Dover Without Perks," the suspects are all rather poor, many of whom are living in government-provided housing. As the investigation takes place on a Thursday and people get paid on Friday, everybody is out of money, and nobody provides Dover with free goodies since they're all scrimping to make it to payday. Porter's social commentary also makes an appearance, as she takes aim at the "caring" community's habit of taking senior citizens and bundling them into state-sponsored housing far away from their friends and family "for their own good" (158-159). Government altruism leads to loneliness that borders on solitary confinement for one sympathetic, sharp elderly woman who has fallen victim to the rearrangement schemes of the official social planners.

Without free food to distract him, Dover has to look into the death of a resident who's been run over by a car and then bludgeoned. After interviewing an elderly woman whose television-watching was interrupted by an annoying burst of static, the detectives eventually realize the cause of the disruption and solve the case. Porter's omniscient narrator notes that both Dover and MacGregor would later claim to have made the critical realization at the same time, but it is Dover who first voices his conclusions, and it is Dover's bullying of the suspect that leads to a confession (171). In the end, Dover manages to wheedle one unexpected alcoholic perk out of the killer before making an arrest.

Dover and the Smallest Room (1979)

Once again, Dover's case is resolved by a great reckoning in a little room—the bathroom. A notorious lothario has a reputation for seducing women regardless of their relationship status, and when a bullet ends his lechery, the main question is whether he was killed by one of his conquests or by a jealous husband or boyfriend.

The central clue is a missing postcard. The victim lined his bathroom with picture postcards, most of which were cheap and tawdry, and the victim's aunt is disgusted by the fact that someone stole the nicest postcard in the place. After she manages to remember where the postcard was sent from and the message on it, Dover immediately puts two and number one together, and after deducing what must have happened and going over the suspect list, figures out who did the crime and why.

Sweating It Out with Dover (1980)

On the hottest and stickiest day of the year, Dover and MacGregor are called to a house in the almost-countryside (though it is surrounded by farmland, it is still quite close to the city) to investigate the death of a workman hired to dig up a small orchard and turn it into a vegetable garden. The owners of the property are a fifty-something man and his supposed wife, who is half his age. The union was never made legal because the man's first wife ran off and refused to let her husband get a divorce.

The victim, who was run through with a pitchfork, had an extensive criminal record and stole all of his gardening supplies from his employer. MacGregor suspects that either one of the victim's criminal associates or the angry employer is behind the crime. Dover, who has kept himself well hydrated with cold beer, uses the facilities and explores the house and grounds a bit, and figures out the killer's identity and motive, much to MacGregor's chagrin.

Dover Sees the Trees (1982)

Despite being published after 1980, "Dover Sees the Trees" and both of the other stories printed after that date must be set before the last Dover novel, *DBB*, because Dover is still "Detective Chief Inspector," and there is no mention of his promotion. Of course, one thing or another could potentially have caused his new rank of Detective Sergeant to fall through, but the means by which Dover received that promotion makes that possibility unlikely.

In "Dover Sees the Trees," a birthday party for a family

patriarch ends in murder. Surprisingly, it is not the wealthy head of the family who feels the pointy end of a bayonet, but rather the young relative from Australia that no one had ever met. Partly to spite the family members he despises, the crotchety patriarch made the grandson he'd never seen his primary heir. With the young man—who turned out to be a loutish motorcyclist—out of the way, the remaining family members are all jockeying to get a larger share of the will and perhaps be named the next leader of the family business.

In the end, Dover does not solve the mystery so much as he is present when the killer spontaneously yet obliquely confesses in order to show off just how clever he or she has been, and it is left unclear whether or not Dover made the effort to find the evidence to make the case, or if he decided to let it go. In any case, the killer's egomania and desire for recognition indicate that justice might come sooner rather than later.

Dover Weighs the Evidence (1982)

In this story, Dover and MacGregor investigate the death of a supposed faith healer who has died after taking a tumble down a flight of stairs. The death may have been caused by a string drawn across the top of the stairwell, and the investigators look into the dead man's neighbors and patients to see who might have wanted him dead.

The most notable aspect of the story is the fact that Mac-Gregor solves the case all on his own, and even manages to convince Dover he is right. Unfortunately for MacGregor and the interests of justice, immediately after accepting Mac-Gregor's summary of events, Dover decides to close the case, determining that there is no evidence to prove the killer's guilt, and no amount of digging is likely to change that. Dover's conclusion is due in part to his natural laziness, and partly due to his resentment at MacGregor for successfully solving the case. In the end, Dover justifies his giving up by arguing that the killer's future actions are bound to lead to an alternative form of justice in the end.

A Souvenir for Dover (1985)

Upon reading the final Dover short story, readers are bound to get a sense of déjà vu, as it is essentially a reworking of "Dover Sees the Trees," with the primary difference being that the head of the family business is the family matriarch, and the business specializes in toilet paper with interesting things written on it, which gives users something to entertain themselves with while they're in the bathroom. The solution to the case is exactly the same as in "Dover Sees the Trees," although in "A Souvenir for Dover," Dover figures out the truth on his own, and may parlay his identifying the murderer into a career in the private sector, even though it is highly unlikely that the killer will ever be charged. Given the aforementioned timeline issues and Dover's previous failed attempts to land himself a cushy job in security, Dover's fans can justifiably conclude that Dover's attempt to obtain a lucrative position may have fallen through after the story's conclusion. After all, MacGregor is unlikely to be lucky enough to have his longtime wish to be free of Dover come true.

Assessment

All of these short stories are solid mysteries, yet they all seem to have reached their proper length. The problem with many novels by second or third-rate crime writers is that they take a simple plot that could be told effectively in twenty to thirty pages and stretch it out to two or three hundred pages, filling the extra space with pointless interviews, side investigations, and subplots that have nothing to do with the case being investigated. Skilled crime authors know how to craft a plot where each scene of a novel has relevance to the unfolding narrative, and each character plays a part more important than red herring. Casual readers often overlook the fact that crafting a mystery short story is often quite different from the creation of a novel. Not only must the narrative take less time to reveal the clues, but there is far less of an opportunity to develop the characters of the suspects. It is not enough to edit a novel aggressively down to size, the scale and goal of a mystery short story must be carefully planned to be a balanced miniature.

Porter knew what the genre needed, and managed to craft stories with a smaller, more manageable set of suspects, and twists that were worthwhile yet required far less delving into sordid pasts and hidden secrets than the motives of her novels did. She found a setting, developed it in a few brief flourishes, and created a handful of suspects. Some appear so briefly as to be nonentities, whereas others are made distinctive by Porter's trademark flair for portraying eccentricities and grotesqueries. Often, Porter's best characters stand out because of how humorously their flaws are laid bare to the world. In most of these novels, the killer never has more than a page or two to be developed, and most have far more to say after being unmasked as a murderer than before the accusation!

Just as characterization is shrunk down for Porter's short stories, plotting must be abridged too, or perhaps better yet, restructured altogether. Arguably two of the best of these mysteries, "Dover Does Some Spadework" and "Sweating It Out With Dover," succeed so well in part because their narratives are plotted so differently from the standard novel. Most of the short stories follow the novel's standard plots—Dover and MacGregor are called out to a case in a setting marked by the quirky behavior of its residents, they learn the facts of the case and interview the suspects one by one, a side investigation or diversion punctuates the line of interrogations here and there, and after a little more digging and questioning, either inspiration or luck strikes and the killer is revealed.

"Dover Does Some Spadework" triumphs because it eschews the standard central plotline of interviewing the suspects, and opens with a humorous look at the dysfunctional Dover marriage, and centers around Dover and MacGregor making seemingly logical deductions. The ending may be anticlimactic, but it is fitting, properly humbling, and gives even more insight as to why Dover concluded long ago that putting a lot of effort into investigating does not pay.

Comparably, "Sweating It Out With Dover" features very few suspects and plenty of boorish behavior on the part of the corpulent Detective Chief Inspector. The narrative does not feature interviewing suspects one by one, but instead covers a conversation with the people who discovered the body. "Sweating," like many of the stories in the anthology, is a case where the solution cannot be determined by studying the clues and eliminating impossibilities, but instead comes from lateral thinking, outside-the-box imagination that leads to an "aha!" People with creative and flexible minds are likelier to solve many of these short mysteries, like "Smallest Room" and "Dark Lady." However, the keenest readers (or perhaps those who have seen these solutions used before in other stories or television episodes) may spot the solution right away, which would make the reading experience substantially more tedious over the course of an extended novel, though the short stories are just about the right length for crimes that can be solved by figuring out a puzzle more than performing an extended analysis of facts and contrasting witness statements.

All of these stories feature typical Dover behavior, which is to say, shockingly bad behavior. His laziness, greed, short-temper, and unpleasant demeanor feature prominently in each story. MacGregor is on occasion sharper (or at least luckier) than he is in the books, and the short stories show the odd couple of detection doing some of their best work as a team.

II

Part Two

Eddie Brown: The World's Most Reluctant—and Hapless—Spy

Eddie Brown

Very likely by design, Eddie Brown is the anti-James Bond. He is certainly not dashing. He is not particularly brave, though he has certain moments of heroism from time to time. He is not driven by a selfless love of his country– he is consistently dragged into missions against his will, signing on only due to threats or pressure. Despite his protestations to the contrary, he is not an especially handsome man. He considers himself reasonably attractive, though many of the women he comes across take him down a couple of notches without hesitation. He is mildly overweight, a point he sometimes concedes and often denies. He is nowhere near athletic, though he is capable of exerting himself further than he ever dreamed possible. And he is not especially skilled at spycraft, either. None of his missions turn out the way he intends them to, although in all fairness, more often than not the situations he faces are far beyond his control.

In spite of his numerous shortcomings, he is not an incompetent spy. He is certainly far from the best secret agent on the Queen's Secret Service, but he is capable of coming up with an effective plan at short notice (although he constantly misses important points that could spell disaster down the line), and when he puts his mind to it he is capable of considerable courage and bouts of ingenuity. He is also reasonably attractive to certain kinds of women, and he either seduces or is seduced by a small handful of ladies over the course of the series, only a few of whom have ulterior motives in sleeping with him. When he fails, it is often due to plain bad luck, although occasionally his unreliable memory plays a role, or simply poor planning from a hastily put-together strategy. He is not corrupt or cowardly, and once his initial reluctance is overcome and he is inextricably immersed in a mission, he throws himself into the situation wholeheartedly, and makes a genuine effort to succeed.

Eddie Brown could therefore be graded a "B" level agent if the person judging him is feeling supportive, a "C" level agent if the judge is not feeling so lenient. He is not a master spy, but neither is he a total blunderer. He is, quite simply, a man who never wished to become a secret agent, but who was dragged into the business against his will simply because he bore a striking resemblance to a Soviet agent. That is all—no great ability or powerful origin story, just chance, and mostly bad luck at that. As the series begins, he is living a quiet life of disappointment, as his skill with languages has led only to an unfulfilling career as a teacher at a third-rate school filled with delinquents. He does not wish for a more adventurous life, but his love life consists of a tepid relationship with a woman he does not love, and he is plagued by a general sense of his life not meeting up with his expectations. Overall, he's haunted by the possibility that perhaps there is something more. Like many others in real life, Eddie finds that an attempt to achieve heroism often leads one far from happiness.

Aside from the genre shift from humorous whodunit to "light-hearted thriller" (to borrow a classification term from

Agatha Christie), there are two major plotting points that separate Eddie's adventures from those of Dover and the Hon Con. The first is the fact that Eddie is for most of his career a lone wolf. The second is narration.

Other than Eddie, the only prominent recurring character in the series is Sir Maurice Drom, a longtime bureaucrat of dubious competence running a secret branch of the U.K.'s intelligence services. There is no "Holmes and Watson" relationship between the two as there is between Dover and MacGregor or the Hon Con and Miss Jones. Sir Maurice never joins Eddie on his adventures, and simply shows up for an extended cameo at the beginning of every book, occasionally appears at the end, and in at least one instance, has a brief telephone call Eddie in the middle of the adventure. The two never work as partners, and it is clear that Sir Maurice holds all the power in the relationship. Indeed, the only reason why Eddie embarks on his adventures in espionage in the first place is because Sir Maurice pressures him with either threats to his livelihood or financial concerns.

Eddie really is the world's most reluctant spy, and he is never too proud to turn to begging or manipulation or jocularity in an attempt to escape the duties of his job. His determination to succeed in his missions is propelled by a desire to preserve his own skin, as well as his attempts to avoid the vengeful wrath of Sir Maurice. Eddie is not propelled by patriotism, idealism, or a desire for personal glory. He has been drafted into the world of espionage, serving his country because he is compelled to, rather than because he wants to do so.

In the last three books, particularly *NCNP*, Eddie's adventures become less seriously suspenseful and more farcical. Murphy's Law tends to prevail in every circumstance– when-

117

ever it is possible for the situation to take a wrong turn, it does, and Eddie is consistently caught up in situations that are comical to the reader but humiliating to him. Often, he has to degrade himself or place himself in an uncomfortable position in order to escape a life-or-death situation.

Eddie's romantic life is also at a distinct variance from that of James Bond. Though he does enjoy the company of attractive women, and does have intimate relations with a few of them over the course of his saga, often the women he beds are the ones he is least attracted to, and he pursues them mainly due to concerns connected to his missions. Also, after getting to know him, with one notable exception, the women in Eddie's life develop a powerful and lasting sense of contempt for him.

Just as people definitely do not want their police officers to be like Dover despite enjoying reading his adventures, sensible people will not want their foreign intelligence services to be filled with agents like Eddie Brown, though it is difficult to shake the feeling that perhaps there are more Dovers and Eddie Browns in public service than one would like to admit.

Chapter Twelve: Sour Cream with Everything (1966)

The Plot

(Note: the Dover and Hon Con mysteries are whodunits, and synopses of these books are easily crafted to avoid spoilers. In contrast, the Eddie Brown stories are thrillers, and important plot details and revelations have to be spoiled so as to make a summary of the plot intelligible. Otherwise, the synopsis would make no sense.)

Eddie Brown is an intelligent fellow who is not anywhere near where he'd like to be in life. He has earned degrees in Russian with top-notch marks, but he is holding down a job as a schoolteacher at an establishment where the students show far more aptitude for brawling than learning. The student body has far more hoodlums than scholars, and as Eddie looks at numerous men his age accomplishing far more with their lives than he has, even though in his estimation they are not nearly as intelligent as he is, he realizes that he is not living up to his potential.

So when Eddie is offered an exciting new job, one would

think that he would jump at the chance at escaping the chalkboards and violent students, but Eddie is the sort of fellow who has a healthy dislike of danger, and though he'd love a more prestigious and lucrative job anywhere else, when a mysterious man tries to recruit him for intelligence work, Eddie balks. Despite his general dissatisfaction with his lot in life, Eddie is reluctant to switch to an espionage career, and when the agent's cajoling proves fruitless, he turns to threats, which prove more effective in getting Eddie to acquiesce.

Eddie is then introduced to Sir Maurice Drom, the director of the Special Overseas Directorate, better known as S.O.D., a not particularly well-respected branch of the British Secret Service. Sir Maurice informs Eddie that he is in the middle of a particularly difficult mission. He has an asset named Anatoly Mixailovich Babak, a Soviet citizen who has been working for the United Kingdom, who needs to leave the Soviet Union and come to England for a full debriefing. The problem is, Babak cannot exit the country without being caught and detained, so Sir Maurice comes up with a plan. Babak has an upcoming appointment at a rest home to recuperate from a nervous breakdown caused by overwork, and Sir Maurice suggests that a substitute stay at the rest home, where no one is likely to recognize him, for just under a month while Babak has his rendezvous with the S.O.D. After his release from the rest home and Babak's return to the U.S.S.R., the substitute and Babak will switch places again, and the substitute will return to the United Kingdom.

Sir Maurice's plan is for Eddie to play the role of the substitute. After running a computer search for people who fit the description of his asset, coupled with people who speak Russian, there was only one man who was a perfect match:

120

Eddie. And so, with promises of a comfortable and glamorous career awaiting him after completing this one assignment, which Sir Maurice assures him will be more of a vacation than a pulse-pounding adventure, Eddie quits his job, abandons the fiancée he doesn't really care for, and signs up for a few months of training at a school for spies, cleverly disguised as a lunatic asylum. After learning some basics in self-defense (and suicide if things go wrong), and a forcible nose job to make him look more like the man he's impersonating, Eddie is on his way to the Soviet Union.

Under a pseudonym and with a S.O.D. agent posing as his wife, Eddie travels through Russia to the rendezvous point, takes the place of his target, and makes his way to the rest home. There, he meets a mix of people, a few of whom are surprisingly friendly to him, such as Melkin and Azatov, both seemingly genial men who later are revealed to be hiding major secrets.

Everything seems to go fairly smoothly until Eddie suspects one of his fellow rest home residents to be a member of the Soviet secret police. Egged on by the contacts Sir Maurice directed him to in case of emergencies, Eddie is convinced that the only way to survive is to kill the man he believes is a spy on his trail, and he does. When later, a rest home employee starts to take a seemingly excessive interest in Eddie, his supposed allies pressure him to kill her as well. This time, Eddie balks, and when the situation seems to resolve itself without his interference, he is relieved at not having to resort to lethal force again. Violence does not agree with him.

Eventually, his month at the rest home is up, and he arrives at the rendezvous point to make the second switch and head home, only to be stood up at the train station. After a long

121

wait, a worried Eddie starts to leave, only to be met by one of his "friends" from the rest home, who reveals himself to be a member of the secret police, and explains that the Soviet spies knew all about the switch from the beginning and that Babek was a double agent working for them. Eddie is offered one chance to get home. The price of his safe return is his committing a murder in Moscow. Eddie agrees but decides to pull a double-cross.

In Moscow, Eddie comes across a gang of Soviet government-paid protestors who were about to hold a demonstration at the French embassy, and after waving a set of stolen credentials, convinces them to protest at the British embassy instead. In the midst of the melee, Eddie breaks into the embassy, reveals his true identity, and demands sanctuary.

Unfortunately for Eddie, no one in the British government is happy that he managed to make his way to safety. The protestors caused tremendous damage to the British embassy, the Soviets want Eddie handed over to them for murder, and in the wake of the uproar Sir Maurice is forced to break all protocol and recognize Eddie as one of his agents. As it turns out, Babek was a triple agent working for Britain, and Eddie realizes to his horror that there were never any plans to get him home.

With no allies and many enemies, Eddie is stuck in a small room in the British embassy, holding onto sanctuary by a single lucky thread. Having nothing else to do with his copious spare time, he explains that he has written the book that the reader has just finished.

Assessment

This is Porter's first non-Dover novel, and it's clear that she was adjusting to the new format. The tone and pacing are far more serious than most of her other works, and instead of being a comic spy thriller like the other three entries in the Eddie Brown series, it is more of a light-hearted thriller with frequent comic lines. Porter was venturing out into new territory here, as all of her previous novels were Dover mysteries. While Porter mastered her personal style for whodunits quickly, swiftly developing a knack for figuring out how to plot her stories effectively and weave the clues neatly into the narrative, switching over to the world of comic espionage required a little more experimentation to make the genre her own.

Porter clearly studied her own writing and realized what did and did not work. Her next Eddie Brown novel identified and corrected all of the problems and shortcomings from *SCE*. *SCE* is a solid book, but there are many facets of it that could use improvement in order to make the story work more effectively. One of the major issues with the pacing of the narrative in *SCE* is the fact the first act of the book is heavy on exposition. Porter wisely kept the narrative of *D1* flowing swiftly by avoiding a lengthy introductory scene where Dover and MacGregor are first introduced. The reader is informed of their exploits and the status of their relationships in a matter of paragraphs. With just a quick reference to a disastrous early case and a brief glimpse at the pair's contentious working relationship, the reader knows everything they need to know about the pair in less than three pages. Even the best writers are subject to the threat of excessive exposition in the first book in the series. Porter refined her skills, summarizing everything relevant about the previous adventures and Eddie's backstory into a few concise paragraphs in each of the later books. A reader can pick up a book at any point in the series and learn everything one needs to know about Eddie's backstory and his personality, though the ending of the preceding novel is usually spoiled to some extent.

Another problem with the book has to do with the characterization of Eddie. Part of Eddie's whole persona is the fact that he is *not* a proper spy. He is not cut out to be sent on missions as an assassin or a disruptor, he is meant to serve as an impersonator or possibly a delivery boy. He is an ordinary fellow who is in over his head. He can usually find a way out of trouble, but he generally winds up creating a lot more friction than he resolves. To make Eddie a comic grotesque, she had to make him a blunderer, but to make him a relatable figure the reader can root for, she also had to make him competent to a limited extent. It is one thing for Eddie to be caught in a tricky situation where no one is seriously harmed, but killing darkens a character. Eddie's one foray into lethal violence, which is a pivotal moment in *SCE*, is not repeated in later books. Not only does denying Eddie a license to kill take away his character's sharp edges, but it also makes him appear purer compared to his opponents who will not hesitate to use deadly force. Aside from a fleeting reference to his taking a life at the start of *CC*, Eddie's lone successful assassination is never mentioned again. The killing of a believed enemy was a characterization mistake that Porter could not take back, but she could ignore it in later books.

Similarly, Eddie's romantic life does not come close to approximating the carnal sensuality of the James Bond novels. Though in *SCE*, Eddie does pick up a girlfriend and catches the attention of at least one other person, his relationship follows a general pattern as mild attraction turns into contempt and annoyance on the woman's part and the individual with an unrequited interest in Eddie is definitely not the fledgling spy's type. Additionally, Eddie's "fiancée" at the beginning of the book is (probably unknowingly to her) only a relationship of convenience, as he enjoys having someone who will provide him with meals, company, and physical gratification regularly, but Eddie feels no passion, love, or even loyalty to her, save for making her the beneficiary of his will, should the worst happen on his mission (12, 37). Furthermore, any delusions Eddie may have that women may find him irresistible are metaphorically put to bed when the spy posing as his wife early in his mission firmly and unequivocally rejects his advances (54).

It is not just Eddie who is relentlessly stripped of all romantic notions of spycraft; as all aspects of sex, violence, and lying are mercilessly painted in the drabbest possible colors. The entire espionage establishment is presented as being far stodgier than the action-packed world of Ian Fleming, and much less competent than the bureaucratic chess-playing of John le Carré. It is unclear how much Porter's vision of espionage was influenced by her own career in the business, as most of the information about her career is probably still classified, and she never went into details about her work, save for one point that was placed on a dust jacket and turned into a major plot point in *NCNP*. The British Secret Service is not depicted as utterly incompetent, but it is presented as being extremely fallible and not nearly as effective and clever as it thinks it is. Comparably, the Soviet spies are often several steps ahead of Eddie (it is ambiguous as to whether the Soviets have seen through the British's machinations or if the British have anticipated their moves and are double- or triple-bluffing).

Indeed, by the end of the novel, while the British have achieved some of their objectives, it is not certain whether or not they have actually obtained any useable intelligence, and given the unfortunate expenditures and embarrassments inadvertently created by Eddie, it is quite possible they wound up falling behind in the whole affair.

While the British spies are not especially adept or reliable, Eddie is at least trying his best, Sir Maurice's heart seems to be patriotic and in the right(ish) place even if he treats Eddie as a disposable pawn, and the British agents (who are not secretly working for the other side) who appear briefly are mostly competent. Eddie and Sir Maurice are far and away the best-developed characters, as the rest of the significant characters are mostly examples of Porter's well-crafted miniatures. The British agents are not perfect, but they are serving their nation to the best of their ability, although often their best is not nearly good enough. In contrast, the Russian agents we see are corrupt, indifferent towards human life, adulterous, and cruel beneath an urbane exterior. The British are often ineffectual, but in Porter's depiction, they are still the good guys, even if they are exceptionally flawed heroes. This geopolitical worldview would continue in later Eddie Brown novels, where the Soviet bureaucracy, brutality, and worldviews would be relentlessly lampooned and exposed to ridicule.

Porter strips the glamour from spy work, and she also makes it clear that British citizens ought to be applying just as much healthy skepticism towards those in the espionage business as they should towards their police officers. While never becoming ham-handed in her critique of international politics, Porter would sharpen her criticisms of spycraft in the

next three novels, where she would make sharper criticisms
through increasingly barbed and sublimely ridiculous humor.

Chapter Thirteen: The Chinks in the Curtain (1967)

The Plot

A s *CC* opens, Eddie has finally been released from his captivity at the British Embassy in Moscow after a year of uncertainty, and he is looking forward to accepting a generous remuneration for his services and starting the nice, cushy job he was promised when he agreed to work for S.O.D. Right after he starts talking to Sir Maurice, Eddie realizes with a heavy heart that his future is not going to unfold as smoothly as he had hoped. Sir Maurice immediately begins upbraiding Eddie for not sticking to the plan and for committing an act of lethal violence, ignoring Eddie's defensive argument that he believed that he had no choice under the high-pressure circumstances.

After savaging Eddie's conduct during his mission, Sir Maurice starts complaining about the massive expenses incurred by the riot Eddie instigated at the embassy, as well as the costs of housing, feeding, and grooming him, not to mention the embarrassment inflicted upon S.O.D. by having to break traditional policy and admit that Eddie was one of their agents.

Given the current government economy drives, there is no way the massive debts Eddie created can be swept under the rug, so Sir Maurice informs an appalled Eddie that the money the government paid into his bank account has been reclaimed and that he will be working for S.O.D. for the foreseeable future as a means of paying off his remaining debt. Before Eddie can finish complaining about the perceived betrayal and his heavily garnished wages, Sir Maurice ships him out on a new assignment, this time in France.

One of Sir Maurice's many projects at S.O.D. is industrial espionage. A crown jewel of his spy networking is a small ring of agents that obtain information on all sorts of scientific discoveries from enemy nations. Sir Maurice is particularly proud of the project that led to obtaining the formula to create a new kind of artificial flowers that wilted just like the real thing, though he cannot understand why consumers didn't want to buy them. Eddie wants very much to complain about putting his life on the line for the sake of items like fake flowers with a short shelf life, but for him, duty doesn't just call, it issues an ultimatum, so Eddie is given his papers, an enormous old-fashioned gun, and is booked for the next flight to Paris.

Eddie is tasked with meeting Sir Maurice's agent Prince Yuri Ivanovich Lavrov, a Russian expatriate living in the Château d'Où, a dilapidated mansion in the heart of the city. The Prince has ceased contact with Sir Maurice, and Eddie has to find out why and hopefully restart communications. The first problem is how to gain access to the mansion. A little digging reveals that Aspasia-Maude, the American niece of the Prince's wife, is visiting her relatives, so Eddie concludes that the best way to gain entry to the Château is by striking up a relationship with the niece.

129

The hapless spy's seduction attempts go far more smoothly than he could have ever dared to hope, as Aspasia-Maude immediately takes a shine to him. Unfortunately for Eddie, she is no longer staying with her aunt and uncle. Desiring her own personal space, she is now living in a tiny garret apartment in a run-down building. In no time, Eddie realizes that he has lost all control of the relationship. Aspasia-Maude is sexually voracious and Eddie can barely keep up with her. When he tries to walk away, she spills coffee all over his only pair of trousers and takes them to the dry cleaners, leaving him with no option to remain trapped in her tiny room. He spends most of his waking hours dealing with carnal matters, and on the brief occasions when Aspasia-Maude steps out to buy sustenance (usually croissants and processed cheese), all Eddie can do is wonder where he went wrong and muse about how unattractive he finds Aspasia-Maude, both physically and in terms of personality.

Eventually, one day when Aspasia-Maude is out, Eddie decides to take matters into his own hands, and sets fire to the apartment building, pilfers a lesbian's trousers without her knowledge, and meets Aspasia-Maude on the street while the other building residents rush out to safety. Having no place else to go, Eddie persuades a reluctant Aspasia-Maude not to check into a hotel, and instead to move back in with her aunt and uncle.

The Château is a massive structure with a giant double staircase, so there is plenty of room for a couple of extra guests. The Prince and Princess Lavrov are not a close couple by any stretch of the imagination. Given the size of the Château, they're able to go for days, even weeks without seeing each other, not that they want to have much contact at all. About the only thing they have in common is the fact that they both like attractive young men. The Prince spends most of his time locked away in his rooms, and the Princess spends a lot of time with her Icelandic gentleman friend, Ari Gundmundson. Eddie learns more than he wanted to about her love life when the Princess beats her niece at a game of cards, and "wins" Eddie's favors for the night, even though he didn't realize that he was the bet. As he is helplessly dragged away to the Princess's boudoir, Eddie reflects, "So unlike the private life of our dear Queen" (64).

Eventually, Eddie gets to speak to the Prince and learns that he has abandoned information gathering for S.O.D., in favor of launching a revolution to oust the Soviets from Russia. Eddie can't get the Prince to provide him with many details, and the Prince seems to be spending more time designing elaborate military uniforms than anything else.

Over the next several days, Eddie meets a close friend of the Prince and Princess, Father Igor Nikolaevich Svolotch (though introduced as "Igor" early on, he is referred to as "Father Ivan" for the rest of the novel), a Russian Orthodox priest who is encouraging the Prince with his revolutionary aims, and who preaches the mercy of God's forgiveness, but adds that, "We must all repent. But how can we repent if we haven't sinned?" (73). Eddie gets a good sense of Svolotch's charisma and ideas of sin when the not-so-good Father leads both Aspasia-Maude and the Princess into the bedroom, much to their delight.

As Eddie tries to figure out the Prince's secrets, he learns that Ari is not Icelandic, but is actually a Russian agent sent to keep an eye on the Prince. He is a former schoolteacher recruited against his will, so since they share a similar background, Eddie and Ari bond and become friendly, despite the fact that they

131

are spies on opposite sides, and decide to work together. For no reasonable reasons other than procrastination and a desire to play his cards close to his chest, Eddie fails to check in with Sir Maurice by phone.

At one point, Aspasia-Maude discovers Eddie and Ari conspiring, and Eddie reveals to her that they are spies. However, to avoid ruffling the patriotic American's sensibilities, Eddie neglects to tell her that Ari is a spy for the Soviets, and instead tells her they both work for the CIA. The trio begin to work together to solve the mystery of what the Prince is doing behind closed doors. Unexplained noises imply that there are strangers in the house, but the trio cannot figure out how they got into the château, since they have been watching the only doors.

The action starts ramping up in the last third of the book over the course of a very tense couple of days. A mysterious man breaks into the house and starts beating up Eddie, but the assailant is stopped by Aspasia-Maude, who shoots and kills him. To his horror, Eddie finds the man's credentials and learns he works for S.O.D. They then hide the body under the Princess's bed (the Princess has been drugged to keep her out of the way), as it is far away from their own rooms, and the one room in the house the Prince will never enter.

As they keep investigating, they discover unmarked maps and a broadcasting antenna in one room. Ari realizes that each map contains the location of a Russian embassy in a different world city, probably for some sort of attack. The trio discovers that there's a hidden staircase inside the main staircase, which is how the Prince's allies have been slipping up to his floor of the château unnoticed. Meanwhile, the Prince becomes more unstable, and locks the trio into a room, threatening to kill them once Father Svolotch returns.

Right before Svolotch arrives, the Prince explains their plans. They will use the broadcasting antenna to send signals to all of their global agents, who are set to release a dangerous chemical into the water supply of dozens of Soviet embassies. The poison is supposedly so potent that if a small amount is swallowed or even comes into contact with the skin, the results will be lethal. When the Soviets find their embassies wiped out, they will respond with military violence against the presumed attacker, the United States, and it will lead to World War Three. The major cities of the U.S.S.R. will undoubtedly be wiped out, but Svolotch and the Prince will take over what remains of Russia, and the Prince intends to make himself the new tsar.

Aspasia-Maude, who does not understand Russian and has missed a lot of what has happened, angrily screams at Svolotch, telling him that Ari and Eddie are CIA agents and that they have passed on all they've learned about the Prince's plans to their superiors. Svolotch becomes furious and barks orders to his associates in a language Eddie does not understand and shocks everybody by shooting and killing the Prince, explaining that he is no longer useful. Svolotch and all of his cronies leave the room, except for one who is left behind to guard the trio.

Aspasia-Maude recognizes that Svolotch has been speaking Chinese, a language she knows since her third stepfather was Chinese. Ari deduces that Svolotch is actually a Chinese agent, probably the son of Russians who fled their home country after the Revolution and started a new life in China. Svolotch was manipulating the Prince. His real goal was not to depose the Soviets and set up a new tsar, but to provoke World War

Three, allow the Soviet Union and the United States to destroy each other, and leaving China free to emerge as the dominant world power.

Time passes, and then Aspasia-Maude shocks Eddie by being able to wriggle out of her chains and shackles due to her extreme skinniness. At Eddie's urging, a reluctant, whining Aspasia-Maude picks up an axe and hits their guard over the head, and after some dangerous chopping, Ari and Eddie are also freed from their shackles.

The trio realize they have to disable the broadcasting antenna and decide to call the fire department and tell them that the château is ablaze, hoping that the firemen will be able to save them, and their ladders will allow them to reach the antenna at the top of the house.

In the climactic scene, Eddie and Aspasia-Maude climb a fire engine ladder to reach the roof and destroy the antenna. Despite nearly falling multiple times and nearly getting shot by the villains, Eddie disables Svolotch and his henchmen with a blast from the fire hose, and makes it to the antenna, but is unable to even put a dent in it before collapsing.

As the novel concludes, Eddie is languishing in a filthy French prison. Sir Maurice arrives and tells him that the authorities killed Svolotch and his henchmen. As it turns out, all of Eddie's efforts were futile anyway, as the poison is far weaker than the villains thought, and cannot harm anybody. Eddie is aghast to learn that he risked his life for nothing, and even more shocked to learn that Aspasia-Maude is being recruited by the CIA, Ari is viewed as a hero by the Soviets, and the Princess has seen the light and is going to spend the rest of her life ministering to the prostitutes of Paris as a Russian Orthodox nun. Meanwhile, Eddie is taking the blame for the fire, the disruption, and the death of his fellow agent, and is now considered an enemy of the nations of Russia, France, Iceland, and China. Displaying no malice, Sir Maurice explains that he's doing his best to get Eddie out, but he'll need to be patient.

In the closing lines, Eddie explains that he's been in jail for six months, and he has filled his days by writing another book about his misadventures, the very book that the reader has just finished.

Assessment

CC is Porter's first foray into crafting a full-fledged farce. The plots of the early Dover novels were bound by the limits of police procedurals, which required the narrative to largely consists of the detectives interviewing one suspect after another, punctuated by conversations where they discuss their theories on the case, plus the occasional scene where Dover causes a ruckus due to his dissatisfaction over his accommodations. There is plenty of humor; largely in the form of comic dialogue, droll characters, and awkward situations, but the ultimate structure of the plot was largely set in stone: a standard police investigation.

The Eddie Brown novels, dealing in espionage rather than a murder inquiry, are allowed to go in a much different direction. Whodunits in the Dover mold must follow a set pattern, where a crime occurs, the detectives gather information mainly by questioning suspects, and the ending culminates in the identification of the criminal. Most of the Dover novel settings are limited to a single village, though in several instances the investigation requires a road trip to obtain crucial clues. Eddie Brown novels have a lot more freedom in their narrative structure. At the beginning of each novel, Eddie is pushed against his will to perform a task for the government. In *CC*, the goal is to learn why an intelligence asset has gone M.I.A., and ideally bring that man back into the spying fold. There are multiple ways that Eddie could have made contact with the Prince, and potentially infinite paths that the narrative could have taken after that point. The lack of plot structure facilitates farce, as the fact that anything can happen means that there are fewer limits to the storyline. Eddie can be allowed flexibility with his mission without a set plan, far more characters can turn out to be villains than in most whodunits, and the narrative can be driven by completing a series of tasks and challenges, rather than by questioning suspects for information. Additionally, the need for careful clueing being introduced into the plot is diminished, though hints and foreshadowing may be sprinkled here and there, though this is not always necessary or even desirable. The spy thriller writer may benefit from punctuating the narrative with sudden shocks and surprise twists that catch the reader off guard, but the whodunit writer will earn the ire of readers if the author does not abide by the rules of fair play. After all, for many readers of traditional mysteries, much of the fun comes in playing the game, reading closely to detect the clues the author has placed into the narrative, and trying to beat the detective to deducing the correct solution to the case. While many mystery readers enjoy twists, turns, and unexpected denouements, an author who does not provide enough clues to solve the crime or who allows for multiple solutions through poor plotting and ambiguous evidence is unlikely to develop a loyal and devoted readership.

Porter limited her narrative options in *SCE*, by devoting the entire first act to Eddie's spy training, and then setting up a mission at a limited location, where the objective was simply to blend in and avoid attracting unwanted attention. The misadventures and Eddie's constant carping make the storyline entertaining, but it lacked the wide variety of plotting options that Porter provided for herself in *CC*.

CC far surpasses its predecessor due not only to the rollicking nature of its plot and wacky situations, but also in terms of its supporting cast. Aspasia-Maude is not the pliant feminine fantasy of many action thrillers, but instead annoys Eddie at every turn, due to her constant complaining, undercutting him at every opportunity, and refusal to accept his authority. The fact that Eddie claims not to find her physically attractive is yet another reason why she flies in the face of the standard "lust interest" trope for spies. The point is further compounded by the fact that she gains complete control over Eddie during their extended coital interlude early in the novel. Despite being a source of frustration for Eddie, she handles many of the spycraft tasks assigned to her competently and her knowledge of a certain language and French history proves valuable, though on multiple occasions her courage fails her and her frantic paralysis leads to near disasters.

Ari is a likeable character and highly competent spy, despite the fact that he, like Eddie, never wished to be a spy in the first place and is acting under duress. Despite being on opposite sides of the Iron Curtain ideologically, Eddie and Ari make an excellent team, and both contribute to revealing the truth about what is going on, with both using their personal skill sets to lead at alternate times. On the other side, Prince Yuri and Svolotch make for entertaining villains, due in part to their both being utterly deranged, though in different ways. The idea that an evil plot is being driven by madmen makes the stakes even higher, as the Cold War policies of détente and mutually assured destruction depended on both sides of the divide being rational people determined to prevent disaster. Porter illustrates that this entire geopolitical system is bound to fail if either one party or an outside entity seeking to upend the system pursues a policy based on the creation of chaos.

The villains' plan of driving the United States and the Soviet Union to war and destroying each other is unsettling, but it is not outside the realm of possibility. The true case of Stanislav Petrov, often dubbed "The Man Who Saved The World," is living proof of the fact that the plan to frame the Americans for attacking the Soviet Embassies could indeed lead to war. In a widely spread account of Petrov's case by Greg Myre (several basic details are debated by historians), technological malfunctions declared that the Americans had launched a nuclear strike, and official policy required a comparable show of force. But instead of retaliating, Petrov reasoned that the reports did not make sense and held off on a counterattack. It was soon proven that the equipment indeed malfunctioned, and by refraining from another missile attack, Petrov had played a significant role in preventing World War Three (there were other people who influenced the outcome, but Petrov's part is the most well-known). Petrov never received official honors for his actions, but this story shows the fragility of a tense peace (Myre).

One moral of *CC* is that by focusing on one major enemy or problem, a government or policymaker ignores a seemingly lesser threat at its peril. Looking at the role that China plays in

138

the early decades of the twentieth century and may play in the future, Porter displayed more foresight than many geopolitical prognosticators. There is one problem with one of the book's twists. The fact that the Communist Chinese wind up to be the chief antagonists of the story adds an unfortunate ethnic slur to the book's title.

CC successfully blends action with humor, providing both an entertaining adventure and a perceptive commentary on the Cold War, while also hinting that people ought not depend on their governments and so-called "intelligence" services to provide global peace and stability.

Chapter Fourteen: Neither a Candle Nor a Pitchfork (1969)

The Plot

The title of the book comes from the Russian proverb, "Neither a candle to God, nor a pitchfork for the Devil," which is directed at Eddie when people start believing that he's of no use to anybody, serving neither the cause of good nor of evil (174). By the end of the book, Eddie's high opinion of himself is not seriously damaged, though his self-esteem has taken a steady stream of body blows.

At the novel's beginning, Eddie has just been released from the French prison where he has spent six long months incarcerated, and has been taken straight to Sir Maurice. Sir Maurice dismisses Eddie's request for a long vacation and instead informs him that there's a lot of international pressure to hold an official inquiry on his misadventures from the previous two novels. Since Eddie is unlikely to come out of an inquiry smelling of roses and is more likely to be made the scapegoat for everything that went wrong in his last two assignments, he reluctantly agrees to go abroad for the next mission Sir Maurice has lined up for him and wait for all of the controversy to blow over. After Sir Maurice tells him he is off to America, Eddie is bundled up into a tiny American plane.

When the ejector seat unceremoniously dumps him in the countryside, Eddie initially thinks he has landed in the American lone prairie…until the people who come to collect him start speaking Russian. Sir Maurice tricked him, and now Eddie is a guest at a Russian collective stud farm. As it turns out, the farm has a secret. Alexander Nicolaievitch, the farm's de facto leader, explains it is actually a religious sanctuary for Christians of all denominations to escape atheist Soviet persecution. Unfortunately, the safety of its members is now being threatened by Ludmilla Stroganova, a member of the Khlysti sect (a group that does not believe in marriage) who recently murdered one of her former lovers with an axe in front of witnesses. The authorities have an airtight case against her, but Ludmilla demands that the other members of the collective set her free, otherwise an ally of hers will deliver a packet of information to the authorities, exposing the collective's subversive religious activities.

Even Perry Mason could not get the undoubtedly guilty—and clearly unhinged—Ludmilla acquitted, but the collective has a plan. According to Soviet law, a pregnant woman cannot be given the death penalty. The plan is to smuggle a man into Ludmilla's cell, impregnate her, and later, after she has been sentenced to a prison camp rather than death, to stage a breakout. Ludmilla already has nine children by many different fathers, and she has recently developed a desire to have intimate relations with an Englishman after becoming enraptured by the British actor Leslie Howard. This is where Eddie enters the picture.

From that point on, the novel becomes as much a sex farce as it is a satire of how the oppressive nature of the Soviet government has warped society. Despite Eddie's constant complaining, the members of the commune are adamant that he be the one to impregnate Ludmilla, and they have devised a complex plan to facilitate that coupling. A highly unwilling Eddie is dragged into the city, where he is expected to change into a government investigator's uniform in a restroom and then proceed to the prison. The plan goes smoothly until Eddie makes a discovery—they have provided him with a woman's uniform. Ever dedicated to the plan, his compatriots swiftly find the materials to make him up into full drag, and when he emerges from the public toilet, Eddie quickly catches the attention of lecherous men...and a lesbian procurator named Zena. Eddie manages to escape a lot of unwanted advances, aside from those of Euphraxie, his associate from the commune who will eventually become his quasi-girlfriend), and finally makes it to Ludmilla's cell on two occasions, where he performs the duties expected of him, though neither party is particularly thrilled with the quality of his performance. Having done his bit for England, Eddie and his allies hurry back to the stud farm, running into a delegation of visitors from Mali along the way.

Upon his return, Eddie announces that he has fulfilled the job demanded of him and expects to return home. Alexander Nicolaievitch calmly informs him that he's just going to have to wait until they know for sure Ludmilla's in the family way. This will take a couple more months, until the time of her trial. When Eddie's finished complaining, he learns that the collective farm is only able to support itself through the publication of dirty books, including the translation of

English erotic novels into Russian. These smutty tomes have been provided by Sir Maurice. Apparently, pornography is widely popular in the Soviet Union, but can only be distributed through the black market. Alexander Nicolaievitch mourns the fact that they have had to compromise their moral principles for survival but feels that the collective farm has no choice if it wishes to preserve its status as a religious sanctuary.

Time passes, and Eddie and other farm residents attend Ludmilla's trial. Ludmilla does her best to turn the proceedings into a circus, challenging every witness and making outrageous and unconvincing statements in futile attempts to clear her name. Finally, after the inevitable guilty verdict but before the sentencing, Ludmilla abandons all pretenses of innocence but reveals that she is going to have a baby. The collective is thrilled.

With the official birth announcement, Eddie believes that he's going to head back to England, but Alexander Nicolaievitch disappoints him once again. They had not thought far enough ahead, and they now realize that Ludmilla won't go to an easy-to-escape-from prison farm right away. She will probably spend about a decade in a jail cell before being transferred to an open-air area, and she is not willing to wait that long. The only hope is to wait until she is about to give birth, and then break her out of the less-secure prison hospital.

Eddie demands to be placed in charge of the breakout plan, but weeks pass and he is notably short of ideas. Meanwhile, his relationship with his girlfriend Euphraxie is strained by the discovery that the lesbian procurator Zena is pregnant. Eddie knows the kid cannot be his as he managed to escape Zena's seduction attempts without her having any inkling as to his true gender, but Euphraxie does not believe him. Meanwhile, women at the commune who have been trying in vain for a baby start asking Eddie if he would be willing to sell his services for money. He does not accept any of their offers.

Finally, Eddie realizes that they do not need to break out Ludmilla. They just need to figure out who her friend on the outside is and take the packet of incriminating information from that person, thereby neutralizing Ludmilla's leverage. After realizing that Ludmilla has no friends, Eddie deduces that her dangerous, violent children must be the keepers of the documents. He is right, but when Eddie and Alexander Nicolaievitch go to confront Ludmilla's brood, the kids are too well-armed and well-trained to be taken by surprise, and they have a foolproof plan to protect their mother's insurance policy. Alexander Nicolaievitch concedes defeat, but though Eddie is unwilling to surrender the others overrule him.

Responsibility for breaking Ludmilla out of the hospital now goes to the mildly deranged Yefim Vasilevitch who develops a complex full-scale attack including bombs and battalions of collective members. Yefim has an annoying habit of pretending he cannot understand Eddie's Russian, when in fact he always knows what Eddie is saying. In the meantime, Eddie has been sidelined and his relationship with Euphraxie is at rock bottom, and at their nadir, they have switched stereotypical gender roles, with Euphraxie going out to work each day and Eddie fretting over the housework and whining because he feels his increasingly contemptuous live-in girlfriend does not appreciate him enough.

Finally, the news breaks that Ludmilla is about to go into labor, and Yefim's over-the-top plan goes into effect, explosives and all. Amazingly, everything goes off without a hitch, aside from the fact that Ludmilla is still in labor when they break her out of the hospital, instead of just having delivered the baby as planned. Eddie manages to rush her to medical attention in time, Ludmilla gives birth out of Eddie's sight, and they all return to the collective.

When Eddie finally sees Ludmilla's baby boy for the first time, he is stunned to discover the child is black. After denying having any African heritage himself, and noting that none of her other children appear to have any hint of that ethnicity, he eventually deduces that Ludmilla must have somehow had intimate contact with a member of the visiting delegation from Mali. The Mali delegation must have been particularly busy, as Zena, disgraced and banished, has also given birth to a black child.

Despite not being a father, Eddie is compelled to stay in an isolated basement with Ludmilla until the Soviet police have finished their search for her. Months pass, and his colleagues promise him that they are working on plans to get him home, but he will have to be patient. Resigning himself to a long wait with nothing to do, Eddie decides to write another book about his experiences.

Assessment

NCNP is arguably the best of the Eddie Brown novels. A fair case can be made to give *CC* that title, but *NCNP* features more sustained comedy, which is untampered by the real and serious threat of a Third World War. While in the previous Eddie Brown books the comedy came mostly from Eddie's recalcitrance to be a spy, and a few nutty situations, *NCNP* is a bawdy sex farce, peppered with potshots at the iniquities of life in the Soviet Union.

Once again, Sir Maurice's behavior notes that S.O.D. cannot be fully trusted– or perhaps he just really despises Eddie and wants him to suffer. Sir Maurice lies about the nature of the assignment right off the bat, and since Eddie's seemingly genial hosts regularly withhold information from him, the canny reader gets the sense that there's going to be some unnerving revelation about the mission around every corner, and these predictions are routinely proven correct.

More than ever before, Porter stresses the point that Eddie is no James Bond. Throughout the book, Eddie is never in control, and though he has a few brief flashes of intelligent insight, he is an ineffectual planner for delicate rescue operations, an issue that proves all the more disgraceful due to the fact that he made an enormous fuss about being put into a position of power. Eddie never gets the permanent upper hand in any situation, not even with his closest allies. He does not willingly go along with the flow, but he is constantly caught up in a riptide of circumstances. Whereas in *SCE* and *CC* he often took initiative that put him in control, albeit usually only temporarily, in *NCNP*, Eddie never is able to assert his dominance, not when he demands that his supposed friends honor the deal they made with him, not when he is trying to wheedle information out of other people, and not in his relationships with women.

Indeed, despite the fact that the sole reason he has been brought to Russia is to serve as a reluctant sperm donor, Eddie is metaphorically emasculated at every turn, whether it is when Ludmilla denigrates his sexual performance, when his girlfriend Euphraxie loses respect for him and falsely accuses him of laziness and shameless philandering, when he is forced

146

to go out in public in drag, and when he ultimately fails to succeed in the one job is he was recruited to do: father a child. Whereas in the other three novels Eddie's successes, pyrrhic or small as they might be, are due in part to his own ideas and plans, in *NCNP*, Eddie is never able to muster a solid win due to his own devices. Other than making a couple of shrewd deductions about Ludmilla's plans, all of the successes in *NCNP* are due to other people's cleverness or pure serendipity.

Yet while Eddie is largely powerless to change his situation over the course of this novel, he is not totally passive. Indeed, he spends most of the book railing and flailing against the plans and fates that others foist upon him. He never stops trying to change his situation, sometimes through pleading and often through threats that he cannot back up, but nothing he does can end his forced servitude in the Soviet Union. No amount of cajoling will sway the minds of his supposed friends who are willing to keep him a prisoner and even kill him if it would make their own situation more secure. All he can do is complete the tasks assigned to him and wait. There is a lot of waiting in this book, though Porter wisely elects to only spend a little bit of time watching Eddie cool his heels and sulk, flashing forward over a period of weeks or months at a time to the next tricky situation or action scene. The action takes place over a period of ten or eleven months, as the narrative requires the full duration of a pregnancy, so the vast majority of Eddie's time is spent in frustrated inactivity. For a man who has been recruited for stud purposes, he's metaphorically impotent in multiple frustrating ways. Indeed, Yefim Vasilevitch publicly accuses him of sexual impotence, sending Eddie into a rage (53).

It is worth noting that unlike his other adventures, Eddie is

147

not driven by a desire to save the world or thwart the bad guys. His purpose is to impregnate a stranger and save the lives of a group of people who threaten and increasingly annoy him. Eddie's main goal is not to complete the mission given to him by Sir Maurice, but to get home as soon as possible. It is worth noting that he really doesn't have that much to look forward to back in England, just continued indentured servitude for S.O.D. In fact, when he returns home, it is definitely likely that Sir Maurice will swiftly ship him overseas on some new unpleasant and dangerous mission. Perhaps Eddie is driven by homesickness, or perhaps he is just fed up with the situation. Without higher stakes and with the morality of the mission ambiguous, Eddie feels discouraged by his work, which if not exactly pointless, is far less satisfying than other missions on every possible level. After all, the woman he's trying to save by making it possible for her to "plead the belly" is an unstable murderess who's trying to exhort her freedom by threatening the lives of hundreds of innocent people. Ludmilla is definitely not the sort of woman who inspires men to risk their lives, treasures, and sacred honors in order to rush to her defense as a white knight. If anything, rescuing her is a perversion of justice. Certainly, Eddie and the leaders of the commune agree that she deserves punishment, but self-preservation causes the recusant Christians to venture out onto some moral thin ice.

Porter uses *NCNP* to explore the morality of expediency. Throughout history, Christians have had to hide or disguise their beliefs in the face of persecution, whether it was the early Christians taking refuge in the catacombs of ancient Rome, or Catholics holding Mass in secret during the persecutions of Queen Elizabeth I and King James, or Japanese Catholics disguising the art and rituals of their faith as an esoteric form

148

of Buddhism. The issue here is that there is a big difference between simply finding a safe place to worship in the face of persecution, and violating some pivotal tenets of your faith in order to protect your safe place to worship.

As usual, Porter never attacks religion itself, but she does not pull any punches when she satirizes hypocritical or morally compromised professed believers and people who adopt outlandish beliefs in fringe sects. The commune is meant to preserve Christianity in Russia, including some of the more outlandish sects, such as the Skoptsi, a group that believes that all sex is evil and that the only possible way to be saved is to castrate oneself. (When Eddie is confronted by a fervent believer who practices what he preaches, an uncomfortably humorous scene follows as the proselytizer tries to convert Eddie at the point of a blade) (63-67). Yet despite the best intentions of creating a sanctuary, in reality, as one of the commune leaders notes, the groups have had to make so many moral compromises that they're starting to wonder if they can honestly refer to themselves as true Christians anymore.

Alexander Nicolaievitch mourns the situation, saying, "We have survived in a dangerously hostile environment, our members are free to pursue their religious beliefs without too much fear of persecution. But—what have we sacrificed? With all our ideals and claims to lead lives pleasing to God, we finish up by conspiring to rescue a murderess from justice by methods which ought to be repugnant to us all" (132). Whether it is by promoting fornication (to be fair, some of the minor sects do not believe in the marriage tie), being prepared to use violence including lethal force in order to achieve their goals, and by making a living from pornography, it's clear to all that the original intent of the commune has been seriously diluted, possibly beyond all recognition.

While the underground Christians at least have the excuse of needing to do what they have to in order to survive, the communist government, which institutes the persecution in the first place, has no such excuse. With the lengthy searches and draconian punishments for violating the norms of accepted behavior, the Soviets are clearly represented as an authoritarian, repressive, and brutal government. The reader is not shown much actual malfeasance on the part of the Soviet authorities, nor is any cruel character in a position of power shown. The only significant Soviet officials are the lesbian procurator Zena and the judge at Ludmilla's trial, who are portrayed as lustful but not unlikeable and understandably overwhelmed, respectively. Perhaps the nastiest aspects of life in the U.S.S.R. were bowdlerized so as not to dampen the humorous tone.

It is further evident that the members of the commune have been deeply influenced by a communist society that has striven to erase any Christian influence. The commune members refer to each other as "Comrade" and occasionally remark on the greatness of their nation shortly after expressing fear of government reprisals. The members of the commune even happily repeat the dubious party lines about the Soviet Union solving major problems, such as the nation being completely free from race prejudice, unlike England ("except for the Chinese, of course, and they're quite different," Yefim boasts, unashamedly proclaiming his own bias) (211). Porter would later highlight how the Soviets would tell baldfaced lies about having cured social ills in her Hon Con. Novel *PIM*.

While *NCNP* is obviously influenced by Porter's time work-ing in intelligence in Russia, it is unknown exactly how much of what she saw made its way into her book. The setting of the Russian collective stud farm is based on Porter's own experiences, where she was once "a reluctant guest" at a similar location, where she was "entertained with enough vodka to kill anyone but a Russian" (Dust Jacket). That is all of the information provided on the farm Porter visited. There's no way of knowing if the farm actually was a refuge for persecuted Christians, or if they made ends meet by translating and peddling smut. Whether Porter was reporting what she saw or using her fertile imagination, *NCNP* is one of her most inspired, wacky, and irreverent efforts.

Chapter Fifteen: Only with a Bargepole (1971)

The Plot

I n Eddie's last adventure, he has returned home after an unspecified time in the Soviet Union, though it is not revealed exactly how he found his way home. He has been working in the dark basement of S.O.D. ever since his return, and he claims to have forgotten what the sun looks like when Sir Maurice finally calls him back for yet another mission.

This is supposed to be a simple mission. Eddie has to fly to Vienna, Austria, go to number 475 in the Hundemuseum-strasse, hand over a parcel made to look like a package of paper handkerchiefs, and come back. When Eddie tries to write down the instructions, Sir Maurice explodes in fury, demanding that he rely solely on memory. Eddie hopes that he's finally been handed an easy mission, and heads off to the airport, meeting Sir Maurice's secretary along the way, who is cooing over a postcard sent to her by Muriel, Sir Maurice's daughter and only child, who just happens to be travelling to Vienna.

As Eddie is bundled off to Austria along with a group of tourists, he struggles with a couple of unexpected distractions, including an overly friendly elderly man who may inadvertently blow Eddie's cover, and Eddie's own ill-advised attempt to avoid detection by tucking the secret parcel into someone else's luggage. Eventually, Eddie retrieves the parcel and makes his way to what he *thinks* is the rendezvous point, after mentally reversing the relevant number and winding up at 574 on the Hundemuseumstrasse. Not realizing his mistake, Eddie finds himself drawn into a gang of criminals who are employed to kidnap Sir Maurice's daughter!

Eddie joins the gang's plans unhesitatingly, believing that Sir Maurice sent him to make sure that his daughter was safe. The kidnapping succeeds, and Muriel is soon a prisoner. Eddie covertly attempts to convince her of his true loyalties, and after suffering through some disbelief and mild physical attacks from the indignant Miss Drom, Eddie, eventually persuades her that he works for her father, and the two prepare for either rescue or escape as the kidnappers quibble amongst themselves and head to Italy.

When the kidnappers bring Muriel and Eddie to a beach to hand over Muriel, Eddie and Muriel knock out a guard and manage to escape (119). They make their way across the water, and up a series of steep rocks, but Muriel injures her foot, a problem that is confounded by the fact that Eddie and Muriel were forced to change into swimsuits to blend in with the beach. Since Eddie is only wearing a one-piece pair of swim trunks, and Muriel is in a bikini, Eddie is compelled to use the top half of Muriel's bikini to bind her foot, meaning that Muriel insists that Eddie refrain from looking at her as they continue their escape. Eddie repeatedly avers that he has no attraction whatsoever to Muriel and given the reader's access to his innermost thoughts, this is not a case of the gentleman doth protesting too much.

Eventually, the constantly squabbling pair come across a glamorous-looking woman, the Marchesa Elena Tonarelli di Muccio, driving down the isolated road in an expensive car. The Marchesa gladly gives the pair of them a ride back to her villa. Eddie is smitten with the Marchesa, but Muriel dislikes and distrusts her, wondering how she just happened to be there at the right time, and noting that there are no servants at the villa. Eddie pooh-poohs Muriel's suspicions, only to be humbled when the Marchesa reveals that she is working as part of a criminal gang, and is preparing to deliver Muriel to her bosses (145-147).

The Marchesa's husband the Marquis and a Russian Colonel arrive. Apparently, both the Russians and some apolitical criminal gangs think that kidnapping the daughter of Sir Maurice Drom is a profitable plan. They inform Eddie that they have taken over the kidnapping and that they have killed the original gang of kidnappers with a bomb. Eddie and Muriel are locked in the basement, and Eddie's attempt at a bold escape leads to him receiving a nasty beating. As she nurses him, Muriel shows her first signs of tenderness to Eddie.

Eventually, the villains bundle Muriel and Eddie into their car to transport them to an airplane for delivery to a location determined by their bosses in Moscow. The plans are disrupted by a disturbance on the road, which turns out to be orchestrated by the gangster West Hartlepool Joe. The two Italian communists and the Russian spy are thrown into their car and driven off the road into a cliff, and Eddie and Muriel are bundled off into a bus. Eventually, West Hartlepool Joe smuggles them back into England, and after a fortuitous car wreck, Eddie and Muriel escape, run across some farmland, and manage to make their way to safety.

Comfortably back in Sir Maurice's office in England, Eddie expects to get that vacation he has long demanded. Instead, Sir Maurice berates him for his mistakes, points out that Eddie went to the wrong house, setting off the chain of events that Sir Maurice observes led to a great deal of unnecessary death and destruction. When Eddie points out that the fact that he just happened to stumble into Muriel's kidnapping by accident is a bit too much of a coincidence to swallow, Sir Drom insists that coincidences like that are rare, but they do happen.

Eddie doesn't want to argue, he just wants his time off, but he is shocked to learn that Muriel has been speaking to her father about her plans for Eddie and herself. Sir Maurice points out that even though Eddie and Muriel were never physically romantic, the fact that they spent so much time together means that Muriel is now "compromised," and Eddie is now duty-bound to marry her. When Eddie balks, Sir Maurice becomes enraged, but then plays his trump card. Since Eddie no longer has the packet of money disguised as paper handkerchiefs that he was supposed to hand over, he must either repay it or face a potential criminal inquiry. Lacking the funds and having no desire to face prosecution, Eddie turns to Sir Maurice for help, knowing full well what the price of Sir Maurice's assistance will be. Unlike the sticky situations in which Eddie was trapped in the first three novels, it is highly likely that Eddie will be stuck in this new situation for the rest of his life. In a departure from the first three novels, Eddie does not talk about turning his most recent adventure into a book.

Assessment

Eddie's last adventure is a little lower-key than its predecessors, and it is the only one of his missions not to be tied directly to the Cold War. The kidnapping of Miss Muriel Drom is only tangentially connected to Russian espionage, as one of their three gangs of captors are Communist spies, while the others are criminal gangs driven more out of a desire for profit than by a political agenda. While still comic, the tone is not as uproarious as in the previous two Eddie Brown novels. This is due in part to the high body count, as one gang of bad guys tends to polish off the villains that came right before them in a series of brutal attacks. Eddie and Muriel manage to escape their ordeal without getting any blood on their own hands, and the deceased are all villains, but the dramatic loss of life, far exceeding the body counts of the first three novels combined, puts a genuine damper on the light-hearted good times.

Despite the substantial number of violent deaths, the overall tone of the novel is still comic, although the atmosphere hasn't been quite this dark since Eddie killed a man with a sock stuffed with a billiard ball in *SCE*. *OWB* hearkens back to the classic screwball comedies like *It Happened One Night* or *Bringing Up Baby*, where a mismatched man and a woman would be thrown together on a road trip full of misadventures, bickering and clashing all the way, only to fall in love by the ending. As always, Porter subverts the trope and has the pair united, but not by the joyful ties of romance. Muriel does not seem to display genuine passion for Eddie, though she does exhibit spiteful jealousy when Eddie develops an obvious attraction to the Marchesa.

In this book, we also see Eddie admitting to some of his

insecurities and admitted shortcomings as a spy. When he is savagely beaten during an ill-advised escape attempt, he reflects upon the fact that he may not have what it takes to be a master spy. Additionally, throughout the series, Eddie has denied the fact that he is somewhat overweight, despite the disapproving comments of various women. In *OB*, he fantasizes about being in better shape and being "bronzed, bright-eyed, athletic, the muscles rippling under the warm brown skin of my arms and shoulders. Panther-like, with lithe sinewy legs and a pancake-flat stomach," indicating his sensitivity over his physique (117). Outside of his daydreams, Eddie looks nothing like the aforementioned description, and he is furious when others point that out to him. When Muriel points out he's out of condition for a spy, he replies, "Oh, go rot in hell!" (124). Given his frankness the failure of some of his missions, Eddie is a generally reliable narrator, but he is less trustworthy when it comes to some of his sore spots.

Eddie is not the only character with a habit of not telling the whole truth. By the end, there's certainly a sense that Sir Maurice is not being totally honest with Eddie. The fact that Sir Maurice claims that she has been "compromised" by her chaste time in close proximity with Eddie withers like the artificial flowers Sir Maurice was so proud of in *CC*. Even if the Droms' social circle resisted the permissiveness of the early 1970s, the events of *OB* would be classified by British intelligence and no one would ever know that the pair were ever within fifty miles of each other. The idea that Eddie and Muriel would be under any social pressure to marry does not hold water. Coupled with the fact that Sir Maurice has a history of withholding the truth from Eddie, and a theory might be posited that Sir Maurice is simply putting pressure on Eddie to marry his daughter. Given Sir Maurice's long antipathy to Eddie, it seems as if he is biting the bullet in order to cater to his only child's whims.

Muriel may not be the woman of Eddie's dreams, but the pair actually work well together. The pair escaped the various dangers and sticky situations together, often with one covering for the other's shortcomings. Eddie was often the one who came up with a plan, while Muriel's instincts were often far superior to Eddie's, as she detected the Marchesa's untrustworthiness while Eddie was blinded by a crush (141). Muriel is not as petulant as Aspasia-Maude in *CC*, and she is far more kind-hearted than any of the girlfriends Eddie picked up in Russia during either of his excursions there. One might be considered overly optimistic for making such a prediction, but it is possible that the relationship might work out better than Eddie might expect. The pair would certainly squabble frequently, and Eddie's professed dislike for her would certainly be a stumbling block for marital bliss, but with a little effort the union might work. One can never tell what direction a relationship will take (even a fictional one), but it's possible that the ending may not be nearly so bleak for Eddie as it might appear at first.

And so, with the close of *OWB*, the spying career of Eddie Brown ended, not with a bang, but with matrimony. Though he escaped from extended confinement from a British embassy, a French prison, and a Russian basement in an isolated commune, it seems that he cannot escape a betrothal to a woman he does not love. This is perfectly in character for Eddie, as his romantic history is full of disappointments and a distinct lack of attraction and affection on his part. In any event, marrying the boss's daughter may provide Eddie with some unexpected career perks. Sir Maurice is unlikely to send Eddie on any more dangerous missions, as he would not wish to make his beloved daughter a widow. Provided, of course, that Eddie remains on his best behavior and does nothing to alienate his new bride...

One mystery that was never publicly resolved is why Porter stopped writing Eddie Brown novels. Without sales data, it is impossible to know if the Brown stories simply did not sell as well as her Dover books, so a financial motive cannot be explored. Dealing purely in the realm of the hypothetical, perhaps Porter grew tired of the unrestrained plot creation necessary for spy thrillers and preferred the more solid structure of whodunits. Perhaps Eddie's constant whining made novels narrated by him less fun to write. And perhaps spending so many years working for British intelligence, Porter simply got sick of the subject. Unless something explaining her reasoning appears in Porter's archived papers, or if someone close to her happened to know why she stopped writing Eddie Brown thrillers, readers may never know. In any case, Porter had just introduced the Hon Con the previous year and was still finding success with the Dover mysteries, so for the rest of her mystery writing career, with Eddie permanently retired, Porter would alternate between mysteries featuring Dover, and crimes investigated by the Hon Con.

III

Part Three

The Honourable Constance Ethel
Morrison-Burke: The "Hon Con" on the Case

The Honourable Constance Ethel Morrison-Burke

T he Honourable Constance Ethel Morrison-Burke, commonly referred to out of her hearing as the "Hon Con," is, like Dover, a comic grotesque, yet despite having a myriad of flaws and foibles, she also has far more virtues than Dover, and possesses a warmth and inexhaustible energy that Dover does not. The Hon Con is a member of the aristocracy, quite wealthy and living off a substantial inherited income, yet living modestly in part due to heavy taxation, and mostly due to innate parsimoniousness.

The Hon Con is unmarried with no children, and therefore has a considerable amount of free time to be filled. Unfortunately for her, she lives in the small rural village of Totterbridge, where there are fairly limited opportunities for social interaction.* She has tried to fill her days with hobbies, charity work, and social clubs, but she has been consistently thwarted by twin forces: her innate desire to be in charge of everything, and the resentment that her attempts to control and reshape every organization she participates in engenders. Additionally, her well-meaning attempts to make the clubs she joins more interesting often accidentally leads to disaster, such as inadvertently turning a fire safety lesson into a genuinely destructive conflagration. As such, every social organization she joins has either shut down completely or been left a withered shell of its former self, and by the time *RCSC* opens, there isn't a single remaining club left in town willing to have her. As such, her boundless energy has to be directed into some form of activity, and that's how she fell into private detection.

As of January 23rd 2020, the Wikipedia article for "Joyce Porter" does the Hon Con. a great disservice by stating that, "The 'Hon Con' books are even less like straight 'who-dunnits' than the 'Dovers' because while Dover is an experienced copper who has, it becomes clear, a good brain, the 'Hon Con' is an amateur bungler of below-average intelligence. Therefore, her solving each case must be achieved entirely by a happy coincidence" (*Joyce Porter*). This is a monstrous slur on the Hon Con. While it's true that Dover is a sharp veteran investigator whose deductive skills are blunted by his laziness and short temper, the Hon Con. is no fool. She's intelligent, though she often has poor impulse control, and her instincts are often terrible. Her solving of all five of her cases is never due to a "happy coincidence," but by inspired deductions and unyielding persistence, though admittedly in a couple of cases some minor or significant points are resolved through confessions provoked by the Hon Con.'s badgering and her revelation of her deductions.

While the Hon Con considers herself a natural leader in her village, she takes no pains to conform to social conventions. This is most evident in her fashion sense. Many of her clothes are army surplus, including the duffel coat and balaclava that are her standard protections from inclement weather. She cuts her own hair, often using a straight razor to carve out a rough short crop, and eschews proper shampoo. In *WHS*, a supercilious hairdresser asks her if she washes and cuts it with "Carbolic soap and a knife and fork?" (133). She hates wearing skirts and dresses, preferring trousers and other items of men's clothing whenever possible, and in *WHS* goes so far as to wear a suit belonging to her grandfather (33).

She is also one of the first fictional lesbian detectives. Throughout the series, her attraction to comely young women is barely disguised (readers are allowed a glimpse into her lascivious mental processes at least two or three times a novel), and it is revealed in her final appearance that at least one infatuation has turned physical. Yet her only close and long-lasting relationship is with her best friend, housemate, and domestic servant Miss Jones, whose first name is a mystery in itself, but is affectionately nicknamed "Bones."

The question, "are they a couple?" has no definite answer. The pair's relationship is shrouded in ambiguity. Miss Jones certainly is attracted to men, particularly young fellows. On multiple occasions, she is secretly thrilled at the prospect of hostile, muscular youths manhandling her. The Hon Con and Miss Jones never kiss or embrace, though they squabble like a long-married couple. At home, they sleep in separate bedrooms some distance apart from each other. On a trip to the Soviet Union in *PIM*, they share a room for reasons of economy, but sleep in separate beds…until the Hon Con kicks Miss Jones out so an attractive young damsel in distress can sleep in the room under the Hon Con's protection. The pair walk briefly walk arm in arm down the streets of the U.S.S.R., but it is hinted this may just because they're worn out from too much walking and need each other's support (97). They share a hotel room and a bed while investigating a case in *WHS*, but it is implied that Miss Jones did not have a very comfortable

experience, and the shared accommodations were due solely
to a paucity of room in the inn and the Hon Con's penny-
pinching (116-117). Miss Jones is occasionally upset when she
sees the Hon Con's interest in pretty girls, but is this jealousy?
Fear of losing her livelihood in domestic service? Disapproval
of her friend's inclinations? Readers never get a solid answer,
and the relationship between the two women is all the more
interesting because of these questions.

Three of the novels open with the villagers musing that no
one is really sure of the exact nature of their relationship. In
the opening of *WHS*, the villagers of Totterbridge wonder,
"Was it mistress and maid? Master and man? Or were they
just good friends?" (8). What is clear is that the Hon Con is the
one with a firm grip on the purse strings. Miss Jones has no
money of her own, and is completely financially dependent
on the Hon Con for her home and board. Indeed, it is never
stated that Miss Jones is actually paid a salary for all of the
housework she does. The Hon Con never lords her financial
position over Miss Jones, though she does assign nearly all
of the housework to Miss Jones, and the Hon Con orders her
friend around on investigations and domestic tasks, relying
mainly on emotional and psychological manipulation, on rare
occasions bullying or pressuring, usually when someone else's
shoddy behavior has put her in a nasty temper. Conversely,
Miss Jones stands up for herself regularly, drawing the line
on the Hon Con's non-deliberate overworking, and rebelling
against her friend's misguided attempts at economizing on
the housekeeping budget. On occasion, Miss Jones is able
to wheedle a slight bonus for the housekeeping budget as
recompense for the Hon Con's thoughtless behavior. After a
heated exchange in *RCSC* where Miss Jones suspects that the

Hon Con may only be investigating due to a prurient interest in the dead man's mother (the Hon Con insists that she "had never given the woman a second thought. Well—not in that way, anyhow."), Miss Jones triumphs, and "For forgiving and forgetting, Miss Jones demanded an extra pound a week on her housekeeping money and all the Hon Con's wheedling failed to knock it down by as much as a lousy sixpence" (26). In a more underhanded instance in *MHM*, Miss Jones sneakily undercuts the Hon Con's attempts to save a few pennies at the breakfast table:

"The margarine represented a small, secret triumph for her, dating back to the last stringent economy campaign but one which the Hon Con had instituted in response to the ever-spiralling cost of living. Miss Jones had not argued and the Honourable Constance Morrison-Burke was now probably the only person in the country consuming best quality butter under the delusion that it was cut-price, bulk-bought margarine" (129).

Miss Jones tends to look after the Hon Con's health as well. The Hon Con frequently comments, as she does in *MHM*, on her "spare tyre," and tries to keep fit by engaging in athletic activity such as a punching bag and skateboarding (55). The exercise does not seem to have too much of an effect, and Miss Jones constantly has to monitor the Hon Con's diet, to much grumbling and resentment. Additionally, Miss Jones often has to coax the Hon Con to take medicines such as syrup of figs, though in *MHM* she allows the Hon Con a boiled sweet to take away the nasty aftertaste (147).

Of the six major characters created by Porter (the others being the Hon Con, Dover, MacGregor, Eddie Brown, and Sir Maurice), Miss Jones is by far the most genuinely good-

167

natured, the least flawed, and arguably the most loveable. Miss Jones always forgives the Hon Con for her overbearing ways (though given the financial relationship between the two, this may be out of resigned necessity), and Miss Jones always tries to see the good in people. Far more bound to convention and formality than the Hon Con, Miss Jones fights a constant losing battle to adjust her friend's behavior, dress, and appearance.

Miss Jones also believes that it is a very bad idea for the Hon Con to engage in private detection, though she can never stop her or even slow her down. At various points in every investigation, Miss Jones is against her will but uncomplainingly drawn in to assist the Hon Con, sometimes to take care of the tedious legwork and research, but occasionally Miss Jones is drawn into a dangerous situation. Unlike the Hon Con, who is a natural fighter, Miss Jones' natural response to a tense state of affairs is fainting.

We never know exactly what the true state of the Hon Con and Miss Jones' relationship is, but we do know that their connection is far more amicable than that of Dover and MacGregor. The Hon Con is not quite so skilled a detective as she thinks. Though she uncovers the truth of every case she investigates, in two out of five cases it's due more to doggedness and pure luck than deductive brilliance, though in the other three novels the Hon Con realizes the truth of the case through a flash of inspiration. Her schemes to determine information are often excessively complicated and often involve deceptions that could not fool a newborn babe. Worst of all, she has a terrible habit of being a woman of thoughtless action, when it would be best for all concerned if she were to take a couple of moments to think carefully about the potential consequences of her actions before doing anything that might potentially cause damage to property or put herself in the bad graces of the law. As the Hon Con is often horrified to learn at the end of most of her cases, catching a criminal and having the best of intentions is not enough to save you from facing a judge's wrath yourself.

* Totterbridge is a fictional village, though there is a town in the greater metropolitan area of London named "Totteridge," which does not fit the description of Totterbridge.

Chapter Sixteen: Rather a Common Sort of Crime (1970)

The Plot

The Hon Con's debut begins with a sharp blow to her ego. The Hon Con likes to see herself as a valuable and respected member of the community, and when she receives a terse letter informing her that her volunteer services at the local free advice bureau are no longer wanted, she becomes enraged. Her well-meaning nature, forceful personality, and complexly ambiguous relationship with Miss Jones are all skillfully outlined in the opening chapter. Miss Jones reminds the Hon Con of all of the recent mishaps connected with her volunteering, most notably the unrest caused by the Hon Con's participating in finding speakers for a lecture series on controversial topics for seniors. The Hon Con found a doctor to discuss euthanasia... only to find out in the middle of the lecture that the doctor was actually looking for *recruits* for his euthanasia program. As the Hon Con good-humoredly observes, none of the elderly attendees fell asleep during *that* lecture.

Never daunted for long, the Hon Con decides, much to Miss

Jones' anguish, that if the local community doesn't want her to work for their advice center, then she will just start her own advice bureau. Demonstrating her tendency to pinch pennies and squander pounds, the Hon Con rents out an empty store space across the street from the village advice center, puts up a sign, and waits for people in need to come to her. After a few days without visitors, Mrs. Burberry, a grieving mother, comes to visit. Her son and only child, Rodney, recently died of drinking Scotch whisky poisoned with arsenical weed killer, and the official verdict was suicide. Mrs. Burberry, a devout Catholic, doesn't believe that her son could possibly have killed himself, and begs the Hon Con to look into the matter so her son can be buried in consecrated ground and his murderer will be punished.

After initially balking, the Hon Con abruptly discovers a longing she never knew she had for a career as a private detective. Never one to do things by halves, she marches to the local police station and demands to talk to the detective in charge of investigating Rodney Burberry's death. Detective Sergeant Fenner is convinced it was suicide and balks at assisting the Hon Con, so the Hon Con plays hardball, good-humoredly threatening to tear her clothes and scream "rape" if he doesn't let her see the case file. Realizing that even if no one believes her, he will forever be a laughingstock if the Hon Con pulls a stunt like that, Fenner swallows his pride and succumbs to extortion.

Upon reviewing the case file, the Hon Con indignantly realizes that Mrs. Burberry's son was not as good a boy as she was led to believe. He was a repeat juvenile delinquent, who was recently released from prison after participating in the assault of an elderly woman. The victim was raped by Rodney's partner in crime, but since Rodney did not participate in the actual rape, his prison sentence was far shorter than his compatriot's. Even though the dead teenager was not a particularly nice or upstanding young man, the Hon Con still doesn't fancy that he was the type to commit suicide, so she begins her investigation, starting with visiting the seedy nightclub where the victim died.

Over the course of her investigation, she befriends several young hoodlums, and interrogates some morally dubious shopkeepers and the dead boy's morally bankrupt parole officer. Once she is convinced that it was murder and she grows determined to find the identity of the killer, she goes to Sergeant Fenner who gently informs her that all her investigation has done is go over ground that the police have already covered, and that he is still positive the death was a simple suicide. Refusing to succumb to his patronizing assurance, the Hon Con recruits her new juvenile delinquent friends, led by the dangerously amiable Jack the John, and asks them to help her track down her suspect. Amazingly, the gang of rowdy young people uncovers the suspect's address, but they refuse to provide the Hon Con with the information, informing her that they will be blackmailing the killer, and they do not want her interfering. They simply told her of their discovery as a courtesy, and threaten her with physical harm if she tries to get involved. After they leave, a temporarily nonplussed Hon Con discovers one member of the gang who was left behind in her bathroom, and after a few threats involving a hot fireplace implement (none of which are actually carried out, though the Hon Con's lack of reverence for the Geneva Conventions distresses Miss Jones), the Hon Con extracts the necessary information.

Armed with her suspected killer's address, the Hon Con takes Miss Jones (who also believes the boy took his own life) and goes to confront the person she believes is the guilty party. The killer readily confesses but decides to kill the Hon Con to prevent her from going to the police. Through a mixture of dumb luck, blind courage, and Miss Jones distracting the killer with a timely appearance, the Hon Con manages to save her own life and bring the killer to justice, but in doing so causes such a disruption that she is charged with a breach of the peace. Instead of being grateful to the Hon Con for catching a murderer, the authorities are embarrassed at an amateur showing them up, and much to her fury, the court ignores the good detective work she's done and decides to punish her with a two-week prison sentence, while Miss Jones, who is pretty much guilty of nothing worse than wandering into the scene of a potential crime and fainting from stress, is bound over for six months.

Assessment

The Hon Con's debut performance is a fun one. Just like in *D1*, the detectives enter the world fully formed, and with minimal time devoted to exposition. In a few short pages, the reader is provided with the Hon Con's backstory, personality, and foibles. The reasons for her launching her own private investigation are believable, especially given how clearly her habit of getting into trouble and her refusal to let a setback keep her down for long are sketched in the opening scenes. Just like the Dover mysteries, the plot consists of the detective conducting a series of interviews, although since the Hon Con has no official standing, she often has to use deceptive tactics to get someone to talk to her, and at times she is forced to skirt the law in a way that could potentially get Dover or MacGregor fired. Yet the Hon Con's trend towards outrageousness, placed in contrast to Miss Jones' more proper and conventional approach to everything, and the seedy locations she visits with a relatively innocent eye, illustrate how Porter uses over-the-top humor to highlight the problems facing a society she continually portrays as being in decay.

As always, Porter uses wit and silliness rather than shrill invective to make her points about the ills plaguing the world. The sharpest target of Porter's barbed social satire in *RCSC* is the delinquent youth culture. The teenagers in this novel have no respect for the law, their elders, or any institutions, and they are concerned only with their own pleasure and profit. For all their recklessness, brutality, and crudeness, they are not presented wholly negatively. Several are shown to take a shine to the Hon Con and Miss Jones, but this amiability is swiftly replaced with threats of violence when the pair threaten the youth gang's plans to make a quick and easy profit (165). Porter's young delinquents aren't hoodlums with a heart of gold, but rather bad apples with a few bites of fresh fruit on them, between all the spoiled spots.

Indeed, the wild youths are not presented as being wholly to blame for their own behavior. The adults who were supposed to raise them, educate them, and turn them into responsible members of the community have failed in their duty to the younger generation. The mother of the victim is presented as a decent, well-meaning woman, but her love for her son apparently blinded him to his flaws, and she was unable to admit that her boy was capable of atrocious acts. In any case, even a caring pair of parents cannot always guarantee that a child will walk the straight and narrow path. Most of the adults in the teenagers' lives are lechers and petty criminals themselves. Perhaps worst of all is one supposed symbol of authority, Mr. Stark-Denoon, a crooked parole officer who keeps himself in tobacco by confiscating the cigarettes of teens under his supervision (a habit famously mirrored by Inspector Dover), and who turns a blind, disinterested, even understanding eye to the possibility that an adult may be grooming a young man for molestation (119-120). Stark-Denoon waves away this potential sexual abuse with a casual "do what you will, it's none of my business" attitude. With adults like this in positions of influence, is it any wonder that the young people have no respect for their elders and their rules?

The Hon Con is certainly shocked by this behavior, as is Miss Jones. The two are probably the only adult characters in the book to express moral outrage at what is going on around them, and even to attempt to find a way to do something about it. The other adults, whether they are parents, employers, acquaintances, or even police, seem to turn a blind eye, live in denial, or write off these teenage escapades as nothing worthy of concern. Perhaps the fact that the police put more effort into placing the weight of the criminal justice system on the Hon Con for a perceived transgression rather than pursuing the juvenile offenders for their crimes leads to an unsettling conclusion: the authorities fear the optics of letting the Hon Con's actions go unchecked more than letting the youthful offenders go unpunished. The authorities accept the disobedient young people as youths working through their issues, but the Hon Con's investigation is a genuine threat to the establishment.

While the youth culture takes the lion's share of Porter's criticism, the authorities that are supposed to be protecting society and holding together also get their share of upbraiding. In every whodunit featuring a detective who is not a member of the official police force, whether it is Sherlock Holmes, Hercule Poirot, Miss Marple, Lord Peter Wimsey, Nero Wolfe, Perry Mason, Father Brown, Sam Spade, Philip Marlowe, or any other amateur sleuth or private eye; there is an implicit rebuke to the police force that the taxpayers are handing over their hard-earned money to with the expectations that the official investigators will catch the villains and protect the innocent. When unofficial detectives step in to reveal the truth behind an unsolved case, or possibly fixing wrongly solved cases where they must clear the name of an innocent person that the authorities have arrested, it is a slap to the face of the system itself. With all the training, money, resources, and powers granted to the official police force, one could be excused for thinking that they did not need any help solving crimes. Yet individual amateurs, mostly with no assets other than brains and determination, are able to determine what really happened where the leviathan of the state bungles the investigation.

The amateur or independent sleuth illustrates how even with seemingly unlimited resources, the experts can be powerless to restore order to a disrupted world. This is an embarrassment to the officials. Traditionally in crime fiction, if the independent or amateur sleuth is on hostile terms with the authorities, the officials are infuriated and humiliated by being shown up, and often try to destroy the outsider's reputation and livelihood in future installments in the series, such as with

District Attorney Hamilton Burger's longstanding one-sided feud with defense lawyer Perry Mason. For those detectives on good terms with the official police, such as Sherlock Holmes with Inspectors Lestrade and Gregson, or Hercule Poirot's long friendship with Inspector Japp, the official police may often be embarrassed, but there is always respect for the outsider, especially when the independent sleuth declines to accept public recognition for the work, and allows the officials to take all the credit.

The Hon Con is a rare instance of an amateur failing to come out on top after her investigations. Not only does she fail to get any credit (not even a chance to shine as the center of attention as the leading witness for the prosecution at the trial), but she is actually treated as a criminal. Part of this may be due to Porter's penchant for playing with the conventions of the genre, but in the context of the story, it represents an unfortunate trend for people who do not fit in with the certain standards of society to fall victim to a spectrum of humiliations ranging from mockery to prosecution. Rather than admit how the Hon Con succeeded where the official police failed, she is charged for actions that could easily be pleaded away as accidents and self-defense, and she is thereby discredited rather than acclaimed. Additionally, the Hon Con's ordeals point out that in modern British society, a noble title does not get you any respect or special treatment. Just because you do society a favor, one should not expect that the people tasked with overseeing society will show any gratitude.

The reader may be angered by the unjust treatment of the Hon Con, but the reader should also be forewarned so as not to be upset by the solution to the mystery. This is not a "fair play" mystery, where the reader can figure out whodunit by reading the book and picking up clues, as the motive for the crime is obliquely hinted at early on, but the perpetrator's first actual appearance comes very late in the novel. In a fair play mystery, the reader can often put the puzzle pieces together long before the detective reveals the solution. If a mystery writer reveals the crucial clues early in the book and fills the rest of the novel with red herrings and ultimately pointless digressions and scenes unnecessary to solve the mystery, as many second- or third-rate crime authors do, the novelist could have contained the tale into a short story. This is an investigative crime novel, where the novel ends where it does because the detective tracks down the information after a prolonged inquiry, and the story wraps up once the truth is revealed. The reader must therefore mostly follow the investigation along with the Hon Con, and even the cleverest armchair sleuth will be unable to state the name of the killer until right before the Hon Con tracks down the culprit, though the most astute readers will be able to make a shrewd guess as to what the murderer's connection to the victim is. A skilled reader will figure out why the crime was committed and what sort of person did it, even if it is impossible to determine the killer's specific identity.

Overall, *RCSC* is a strong start to Porter's third and final series. The characters of the Hon Con and Miss Jones are well-developed, though while Dover and MacGregor went through their careers largely unchanged, Porter's female detecting team would develop through small but subtle changes and revelations over the course of the next four books.

Chapter Seventeen: A Meddler and Her Murder (1972)

The Plot

As the Hon Con's second adventure begins, the aristocrat is scrubbing her windows and trying to stave off boredom at her. The household chores at her cottage Shangrilah are usually the exclusive domain of the long-suffering Miss Jones, but for reasons that are never fully explained, the Hon Con does not believe that window-washing qualifies as "woman's work," so she's stuck cleaning the glass, though she's not pleased with being compelled to perform this activity.* Looking out the window, she sees a major disruption going on at a neighbor's house. The police cars are lining up, and a small crowd of villagers are watching the proceedings with great interest. Not one to be left out of any excitement, the Hon Con abandons the windows in order to investigate.

Miss Jones begs the Hon Con to stay away from the police, given the fallout of her previous adventure. It is revealed that the Hon Con did not actually have to serve the prison sentence she was hit with at the end of *RCSC*, but only because she filed a successful yet annoyingly expensive appeal. Porter fails to

179

make it clear whether or not Miss Jones's six-month probation was overturned as well. Despite continued beseeching on Miss Jones' part, the Hon Con goes out into the wet weather to try to figure out what's happening at the Hellon house. When the police refuse to accept her as an unofficial partner, and the Hon Con's inquiries at a local bakery near the crime scene prove fruitless, a dejected Hon Con stumbles home, only to be further upset when it turns out that Miss Jones found out far more information than the Hon Con did without even having to leave the house, thanks to her friendship with an egg-delivery woman who is well-connected to sources of local gossip.

The murder victim is Teresa O'Coyne, an Irish au pair girl serving the Hellon household. Young Teresa was supposed to help the Hellons with their new baby, but she seems to have largely taken on the role of a lazy, sullen teenager, only performing household tasks when she felt like it (which was not all that often), and helping herself to as much choice food as she desired. Apparently, Mrs. Hellon was too shy to fire her, believing that poor help was better than no help at all. In any event, Teresa's unsatisfactory employment came to an end when she was knocked unconscious in her own bed and strangled with a scarf. There is no evidence of sexual assault, but it's possible that Teresa could have let her killer in herself.

Despite having no client, the Hon Con throws herself into the investigation with her usual exuberance. Most of the first half of the book is devoted to her interrogating her neighbors for information, coming up with all sorts of different reasons for stopping by, and provoking all sorts of humorously awkward reactions. Sometimes she arrives unexpectedly, bearing inappropriate or upsetting gifts, such as when she ravages Miss Jones' daffodils in order to present a bouquet to people with far nicer blooms in their own garden, or when she decides the best way to charm an elderly and imperious neighbor is to present her with a thermos full of broth made from boiled bouillon cubes and spoiled sherry. Midway through the novel, the Hon Con starts narrowing her suspects and begins trying to break one suspect's alibi, leading to an alliance with an attractive female cab driver (whose existence she tries and fails to keep hidden from Miss Jones), and culminating in wrangling an invitation into the scene of the crime by offering to help Mr. Hellon's mother in any way needed, now that her daughter-in-law is at a nursing home, recuperating from the shock of the murder, and the baby needs looking after at home. Mrs. Hellon the elder jumps at the opportunity to exploit the help of an unpaid drudge. And so, the Hon Con is ironically compelled to exhaust herself by performing domestic tasks, the very drudgery she started her investigation in order to escape. Indeed, the cleaning, polishing, and diaper-changing are a great deal less pleasant for the Hon Con than the original window-washing.

Completely worn out and about to give up hope, the Hon Con unexpectedly but luckily comes across a witness in the early hours of the morning who helps her make a massive break in the case. Rushing to the police station, she triumphantly declares her solution to the crime, thereby astounding Sergeant Fenner. Delighted to see that Fenner agrees with her conclusions, the Hon Con is anticipating kudos and publicity for bringing the case to a triumphant end, only to be shocked and as close to humbled as she can get by the revelation that the police determined the true identity of the killer long before she did (though by completely different means), and were just waiting to tie up a few small loose ends before making an arrest. Robbed of her dramatic success, the Hon Con stomps away and decides to take up a new hobby: starting a women's rugby football team.

Assessment

Despite a great many similarities, *MHM*'s narrative goes in a radically different direction from its predecessor. In *RCSC*, the Hon Con's investigation takes her into the seediest portions of her neighborhood, and she uncovers the violence, dissipation, and cruelty of the rebellious young people who are shaking up the community. The solution to *RCSC* is revealed from the dogged following-up of one lead after another. In contrast, *MHM* focuses on the seemingly respectable adult citizens and their hidden secrets, some of which are relevant to the crime, some of which are not. The narrative deals with social ills that are hidden underneath a thin veneer of respectability, rather than youths in a state of open rebellion towards society. In *MHM*, the Hon Con's inquiries bring small amounts of information here and there, but the case is solved by the discovery of a single clue, which leads to the Hon Con making some intelligent and inspired deductions that lead her to determine the identity of the perpetrator.

There is a bit of ambiguity in the title. Who exactly is the "Meddler?" At first, the answer appears obvious—The Hon Con is meddling in a murder mystery she has no business investigating. As more about the victim is revealed, it is shown how she was meddling in a certain situation that would upend at least one person's life, potentially leading up to her own death. In any case, the Hon Con is certainly meddling by inserting herself into the personal private business of all of her neighbors.

Aside from the Hon Con and Miss Jones, the only characters to appear in all five of the series' mysteries, only a couple of characters from *RCSC* make return appearances, the intimidated police officer Sergeant Fenner and the oily, libidinous hotel manager Mr. Welks, who is, if not exactly openly gay, is about as close to uncloseted as possible. In *RCSC*, their backstory is revealed, as the Hon Con and Welks became pals when they were both enrolled in an art class some time earlier, and Welks demanded male nude models in addition to the female ones. The Hon Con had no interest in the naked masculine body, but ever one for gender equality in all things, took Welks' side. Welks took his protest a step further and demanded a young boy as a model, leading to both of them being kicked out of the class (134-135). As the hotel Welks manages, the Martyr's Head, attracts a seedier sort of clientele, in both *RCSC* and *MHM*, the Hon Con finds that a suspect has stayed at the hotel, and she interrogates Welks for information. It is not explicit, but strongly hinted in *MHM* that Welks may have violated a straight young man after he passed out from consuming too much alcohol (113-114).

The amiable but unsavory characterization of Welks is part of a larger trend in Porter's books. The definite lesbians (the Hon Con, women she's attracted to or have had relationships with in the past, and Colonel Bing and Miss McLintock from *D1*), are portrayed as amiable, kind, friendly, and likeable women. The gay men like Welks, Clifford de la Poche in *DED*, Melkin in *SCWE*, and Lavrov in *CC* are mostly sleazy, flamboyant, potentially guilty of sexual abuse or have a preference for young men or boys. Why Porter consistently crafts these characterizations as she does in unknown.

Most of the other characters have only brief appearances, and Porter depicts them all as flawed people, mostly with more of a touch of grotesqueness to them. There's a couple named Adam and Eve who despite all appearances, are definitely not living in paradise. There's an elderly, imperious woman named Mrs. Urquhart, who takes deep relish in embarrassing the Hon Con for dressing in an insufficiently ladylike manner (69). Other characters embody the atmosphere of the village of Totterbridge, where well-meaning incompetence reigns, and unconscious hypocrisy is the norm.

Porter skewers the attitudes and habits of the townspeople in a passage describing a wretched organic bakery run by two sisters, writing:

"The Misses Miller hitched their star to the natural food bandwagon. It was a shrewd move. The comfortably-off, middle classes of Totterbridge longed for the simple life and spent small fortunes on sets of golf clubs and high-powered motor boats to get it. Lolling in their plastic contoured chairs and staring glassy-eyed at their colour television sets, they pined for the crusty bread and homemade cakes of their youth. The Misses Miller had guaranteed to provide both and for several weeks had done a roaring trade. Who, after all, could resist the lure of patisseries made from flour nurtured only in the very highest grade of genuine farmyard manure?

Well, most of Totterbridge's élite could, actually, though they would rather have died than admit it. Gradually, the swing back to the super-markets began and the sales of nice white sliced bread (so handy) and standard-mix cakes in cardboard boxes (so hygienic and you did know what you were getting) returned to normal. The Misses Miller did not go bankrupt, however, as the adulterated goods could only be enjoyed secretly in the bosom of the family. When guests were present, it was *de rigeur* to serve only the products of Ye Olde Paisterie Cooke Shoppe, thus preserving one's reputation for truly gracious living. There was one unexpected fringe benefit. The staff of life, as provided by the Misses Miller, needed so much resolute mastication and their cakes were so unappetizing that the cost of running a tea party was nearly half what it had been in the bad old days" (16-17).

This clever passage good-humoredly but devastatingly illustrates the social absurdities and innate contradictions that permeate the village, showing how affectations rule the day, and social pressures are applied even when they do not make sense. For someone who does not succumb to the peer pressure easily, like the Hon Con, it can lead to situations where the other villagers would find it easier to ostracize the person who does not assimilate into the standard patterns of behavior, rather than face the follies of their own double standards.

The victim is portrayed unsympathetically. Despite being murdered in her bed, she is revealed to be a gold digger, determined to land herself a rich husband, and determined to use her feminine wiles—and her willingness to withhold her sexual favors until she is sure of her quarry—in order to land herself a comfortable life.

One of the most surprising and revealing scenes comes from one telling passage that sheds some potentially illuminating light into Miss Jones' backstory. As the Hon Con and Miss Jones muse on the background of the murder victim, Miss Jones starts to wonder if the dead girl could have been done

185

wrong by some lascivious man, saying:

"We all make mistakes, dear," murmured Miss Jones, "especially when we are young and where the heart is concerned. Teresa simply wanted to get married. Well, what could be more natural? I expect she longed to have a hubbie and kiddies of her own just like everybody else. Then, one day, she met a handsome young man, perhaps, and fell head over heels in love with him. He deceived her, of course, like men do and pretended that he wanted a sweet little home and family as much as she did." Miss Jones's eyes filled with tears but she choked them back and carried on. "Well, one can guess what happened next. She trusted him absolutely and so, when he begged her to anticipate their marriage vows, she succumbed to his entreaties." It was no good. Miss Jones's feelings got the better of her and she had to break off and make use of her handkerchief. "Some gentlemen can be very persuasive" (124-125)."

Given the emotion that Miss Jones displays during this monologue, one can wonder if she is drawing from personal experience here. If that is the case, given the Hon Con's lack of recognition and sympathy, it can therefore be concluded that this is an episode of Miss Jones' life that she has never shared with her closest friend.

The use of the word "friend" here seems appropriate, as while *RCSC* depicted the relationship between the two women as possibly romantic, a platonic friendship could not be ruled out, and ultimately every scene between them was carefully designed to be ambiguous, though one of their acquaintances over the course of the investigation assumed they were a couple and neither woman made any effort to correct him. It's possible that his references to Sapphic relationships went over their heads– as various scenes in *MHM* show, the Hon Con's worldliness is highly inconsistent. She is fully aware of the goings-on of bohemian so-called fashion models when she interviews the victim's sister, a member of that profession (139). The Hon Con, however, is completely clueless when it comes to Welks' none-too-subtle innuendoes. Miss Jones, comparatively, is much more of an innocent. In the rare cases where she expresses awareness of the sexual permissiveness in contemporary society, she makes it unquestionably clear that she does not approve. When the Hon Con starts theorizing about adultery as a motive, Miss Jones declares, "If a married woman falls in love with somebody else's husband, they both get divorces and remarry and nobody thinks one iota the worse of them for it, except for a few old-fashioned people like me" (151). Miss Jones, it seems, is a kindly prude.

Midway through the novel, it is made clear that the Hon Con and Miss Jones share separate bedrooms. This is shown in one nighttime scene where the Hon Con wakes up in the middle of the night and has to use the bathroom, cursing Miss Jones for foisting cups of bedtime cocoa upon her. When the noise of the refilling cistern wakes Miss Jones and provokes the same urge in her, the Hon Con takes malicious joy in hearing her friend wake up and leave her room (156).

Additionally, the Hon Con engages in a reciprocated flirtation with Charlie, a young woman working as a cab driver, who happily assists in the investigation, and makes it unquestionably clear that she'd like to know the Hon Con more intimately. Nothing serious happens between the pair, but the Hon Con is obviously smitten, and she makes a valiant though ultimately futile effort to prevent Miss Jones from learning about Charlie's true gender, and once Miss Jones learns the truth, her attitude turns uncharacteristically glacial. The amicable domestic camaraderie is only restored by the Hon Con's declarations of intestinal distress over the greasy fish and chips Charlie served for lunch, leading Miss Jones to forget her hauteur and devote herself to nursing a symptoms-exaggerating Hon Con back to health. Miss Jones's reaction may be jealousy, or it may be concern that her friend will provoke a scandal, or possibly even concern for Charlie (130-131).

While the Hon Con clearly is attracted to Charlie, Charlie makes a careless remark that nearly sours the Hon Con's opinion of her. When Charlie declares, "You're kind of a real life Miss Marples [sic]," the Hon Con blanches, for "It was not a comparison that struck the Hon Con as particularly felicitous, especially as she had taken great pains to model herself on an original mixture of Lord Peter Wimsey, Maigret and James Bond" (104).

(Note: the following paragraphs will contain more potential spoilers than the rest of the analysis.)

The closing scene is very much in the vein of some of the Golden Age mystery writer Anthony Berkeley's work, particularly his novel *Roger Sheringham and the Vane Mystery*. In that novel, the titular detective comes up with an ingenious solution to a murder, only to be humiliated when the seemingly stolid and unimaginative police detective disproves his theory and reveals the truth, which is a much simpler and obvious solution. (Other authors have used the trope of the brilliant amateur being humbled by the modest professional, but Berkeley's usage is arguably the most famous.) Berkeley took great delight in providing multiple solutions to many of his mysteries, but Porter takes a different tactic here: in *MHM*, she illustrates two very different ways to solve the same case. This reflects how many readers successfully solve mysteries. Some carefully dissect the books for clues and piece them together, while others go by instinct or recognize tropes being utilized in the novel.

Though the ending is not as satisfying for the Hon Con as she hoped, at least this time the authorities have not tried to prosecute her, and even though the police were several steps ahead of her the whole time and made a solid case without her, the Hon Con did come across a piece of incriminating evidence that will likely cement the conviction of the killer. Still, for the Hon Con, a consolation prize is nothing more than an acknowledgement of the fact that she did not win, and the shock of all of her efforts being proven superfluous are enough to put her off private detecting altogether. Thankfully for her fans, she would not be discouraged from involving herself in cases for long.

* The spelling of the Morrison-Burke home varies between novels, sometimes including an "h" at the end, sometimes not.

Chapter Eighteen: The Package
Included Murder (1975)

The Plot

This is the only Hon Con novel not to take place in England. As the book opens, the Hon Con is in the unenviable position of having no outlet for her prodigious enthusiasm and energy, since her previous attempts to fill her days by joining every local club and charitable society in her village have invariably led to disaster. Since no local organization wants her as a member, Porter's omniscient narrator wryly informs the reader that the Hon Con "finally descended to rock bottom and announced her decision to become a writer" (19). Partially inspired by a desire to opine on international affairs and mostly driven by the cheapness of a packaged vacation to the Soviet Union, the Hon Con, with Miss Jones reluctantly in tow, rushes off halfway around the world in order to observe conditions behind the Iron Curtain and turn her experiences into a book.

The Hon Con's plans for a research trip are swiftly derailed when Penelope (Penny) Clough-Cooper, one of thirteen British tourists on the packaged vacation plan, declares that she's the target of a series of attempts on her life. While the other travelers are reluctant to get involved, fearing that the intrusions of the notoriously untrustworthy Soviet police into the matter might lead to inconvenience for all concerned. The Hon Con, intrigued by the prospect of an investigation, and charmed by Miss Clough-Cooper's youth and beauty, takes the case, attempting to figure out who's behind the attempts on her young acquaintance's life. Miss Jones has taken a sharp dislike to Penny Clough-Cooper, and is increasingly irritated by the Hon Con's infatuation with her travelling acquaintance, even though Miss Jones cannot resist the Hon Con's exhortations to help her with the investigation.

The only suspects are the other tourists, including a libidinous artist and his in-denial wife, a wealthy woman and the husband she constantly belittles, a young man about to begin a career in publishing, and his garrulous mother, a honeymooning couple who can't keep their hands off each other, and a pair of working-class brothers with a fondness for crude remarks an innuendo. Over the course of about two weeks, the tourists travel all over the western portions of the U.S.S.R., battling boredom, discomfort, and officious tour guides, as the Hon Con pries into the secrets of her fellow tourists and the attacks on Miss Clough-Cooper keep coming, growing in viciousness and declining in subtlety. The tourists visit famous sites such as GUM department store, Lenin's Tomb, and the resort town of Sochi, as well as enduring lengthy operas they cannot understand, a constant barrage of Soviet propaganda that fools nobody, and most perfidious of all, notoriously unreliable Soviet plumbing.

As the narrative unfolds, the Hon Con interviews the suspects, the shortcomings and foibles of the Soviet Union are exposed, and multiple additional unsuccessful attempts are made on Miss Clough-Cooper's life.

The Hon Con is at a loss to figure out who's behind the mayhem, but she manages to put the pieces together upon the group's return to England, just as the situation turns truly deadly. And in a triumphant conclusion, the Hon Con reveals the truth and shows up the police. This is arguably the Hon Con's most successful ending of all of her mysteries. Not only does she solve the case before the authorities, but she also escapes her frequent fate of being charged with disturbing the peace. As always, she fails to receive the official thanks, kudos, and honors that she believes she deserves.

Assessment

PIM begins Porter's trend of experimentation with the mystery narrative in the Hon Con novels. After two books following a traditional murder mystery structure, the violent death in *PIM* takes place very late in the story. In *WHS*, the violent death is similarly not revealed until very close to the ending, and it is never made clear whether the Hon Con's or the killer's version of events is closer to the truth. By *CBC*, there is no murder at all, but a very different sort of crime set to take place in the story's final pages.

In *D3*, as stated earlier, the distinct influence of Agatha Christie's *The Moving Finger* could be seen in the narrative, or at least an incredible coincidence was in play. It's quite possible that Porter was once again inspired by Agatha Christie when writing *PIM*, though the solution to the crime has been used by many other notable writers such as Anthony Boucher. Christie found the plot twist so effective that she incorporated it into at least four of her novels. It is a very good one, and a surprising one if the reader is not familiar with it. Veteran mystery readers will recognize it immediately, which means that the savvy reader will identify a villain's identity right away. Once the plot template is identified, the reader will pick up on the clueing, which is steadily paced throughout the novel, with a vital clue or piece of foreshadowing being placed in nearly every chapter. Most of the important information is contained in seemingly throwaway lines of dialogue, which only takes on relevance when the reader knows or suspects the solution.

While the crime is arguably the simplest of Porter's fair-play mysteries to solve, the primary interest of the book comes not from the puzzle, but from the depiction of the Soviet Union. Porter never shied away from skewering the social foibles and institutionalized corruption of her home nation, but in Porter's estimation, England in the latter half of the twentieth century was downright utopian and filled with paragons of humanity compared to the Soviet Union. In *PIM*, the Soviet Union is portrayed as, if not exactly a hellhole, a joyless, bureaucratic nightmare filled with drones who mindlessly repeat the party line out of fear of reprisals. It's a society where life is bleak and danger lies right around the corner for anyone who steps out of line, where beauty and innovation and honesty are in short supply, and while the England of Dover and the Hon Con is portrayed as fraying at the edges, the Soviet Union is depicted as completely falling apart at the seams.

The Hon Con decided to visit the Soviet Union because the package tour was comparatively cheap, and she thought that she might be able to turn her experiences and observations into a book. As the narrative unfolds, it is clear that not a single member of the thirteen people on the cross-country tour is actually enjoying the trip. After all, there's not much to take pleasure in on this trip. Most of the sites they visit are crowded or dirty, and many of the places of actual historical interest are closed when they come to visit. The nightlife tends to consist of long, boring operas that are well-nigh impossible for people who do not understand Russian to follow.

As always, it would not be a Joyce Porter novel without generous servings of bathroom humor, and *PIM* has a running gag featuring the extreme unreliability of Soviet plumbing. In the first instance of this theme, Porter's omniscient narrator observes that "Russian plumbing is pretty noisy at the best of times" (17). As the travelers are shuffled from one hotel to the next, the one constant is that they cannot rely upon the toilets in their rooms to do the job they were made to do. It is a constant source of irritation for the Hon Con, who repeatedly tinkers with the machinery, though the problem is exacerbated by the fact that she does not really understand plumbing. She can take a toilet's internal mechanisms apart, but reassembling them is a bit outside her area of expertise. In one instance, as she leaves the dissembled toilet in a state of disarray, she laughs and tells Miss Jones to "improvise" and "use [her] initiative" (131).

The longer the tour goes, the more desperate the travelers are to get home to the relative order and safety of England. The meals are only served during rigidly enforced hours, so when the tours don't stick to the schedule, as they often do when the guides are disorganized or feeling malicious, the powers that be refuse to feed the weary travellers. The tourists are given the choice of going hungry, paying for an overpriced meal at a restaurant with their own money (an unacceptable option for the Hon Con, who always keeps a sharp eye on her pennies), or the Hon Con's preferred option: making do with a private stash of chocolate (114).

The tour guides all regurgitate the scripts that they are assigned. The half-dozen or so guides all declare that the Soviet society is the best in the world, downplay the fact that religious believers still exist under the officially atheistic regime, insist that the U.S.S.R. has been cleansed of social ills like prostitution, and attempt to bully and browbeat the tourists into submission when they balk or object (36-37, 84-85). The guides' attempts to control their charges are only somewhat successful, especially when the Hon Con seeks to throw her weight about both metaphorically and literally. All of the Soviets are portrayed as being either bullies, corrupt, or callous.

The main reason why the Hon Con takes on the investigation of the attacks on Penny Clough-Cooper, aside from her own love of sleuthing, is the fact that none of the British travelers trust the Soviet police. All of them are firmly convinced that any contact with the official authorities will lead to disaster, especially for the innocent members of the group. The fact that something terrible might happen to Miss Clough-Cooper is tragic, of course, but...given the choice between the potential death of a stranger and being thrown into some gulag for the rest of their lives, all of the travellers save for our heroines unhesitatingly decide that this unfortunate young woman will just have to take the potentially fatal lumps that are coming to her.

The suspects in the novel are all grotesques in their own

195

way, and some of them are developed far more than others. The honeymooning Smiths have very little personality, and all the reader learns about them is that they have trouble keeping their hands off each other. The Lewcock brothers are layabouts who wish to game the system through insurance fraud, and who know an astounding number of bawdy slang terms for micturition. Of the other couples, the men are notably undevoted husbands, and the wives are emasculators who tear down their spouses publicly. As for the mother-and-son pair, the son is high on the recklessness of youth and low on scruples, and his mother is a kindly woman who is prone to hysterics and embarrassing, poorly considered outbursts. Miss Clough-Cooper is far and away the best-developed of the new characters. Her physical attractiveness catches the eyes of all the men (and the Hon Con), but she is not sufficiently charming to make any of them save the Hon Con take steps to protect her. Miss Clough-Cooper vacillates between being a weepy damsel in distress to being prickly and hostile towards the Hon Con's admittedly overbearing attempts to shield her from the unknown danger.

Throughout the book, Miss Jones expresses her sharp distrust towards Miss Clough-Cooper, repeatedly insisting that the woman is lying about her past, criticizing her hairstyle choices, and generally denigrating her to the Hon Con at every opportunity. The motives for the normally sweet and reticent Miss Jones' behavior may be based in jealousy, due to the Hon Con lavishing all of her attention on a comely new face, but it may also be predicated out of concern for the Hon Con, who has provoked many a scandal with her reckless love life, and perhaps Miss Jones just does not want to see her friend get hurt. Miss Jones does not seem to take any pleasure in getting

THE PACKAGE INCLUDED MURDER (1975)

a room to herself when the Hon Con orders Miss Clough-Cooper to take Miss Jones' place in their double room for her own protection one night (153-154). This once again may be due to anger over Miss Jones feeling displaced in her relationship with the Hon Con., but there is also the fact that Miss Jones is fully aware of the potential dangers of sleeping in the room of a woman marked for death. In any event, Miss Jones is thoroughly miserable on the trip, due to both the uncomfortable setting and the cringe-inducing attempts by the Hon Con to serve as Miss Clough-Cooper's white knight.

PIM possesses one of Porter's most obvious solutions, but the trademark humor and sly digs at the many shortcomings of the Soviet Union make it an enjoyable read.

Chapter Nineteen: Who the Heck is Sylvia? (1977)

The Plot

T he latter three of the five Hon Con novels use an unconventional plot structure for mysteries. In *PIM* and *WHS* the mysterious death either occurs or is uncovered quite late in the narrative, whereas in *CBC* there is no murder at all! For most of *WHS*, it seems as if the investigation is simply an inquiry into a case of potential imposture, and potentially a fraud.

As the novel opens, the Hon Con is invited to a consultation over tea with Augusta "Gussie" Ottaway, the eldest sibling of a trio in charge of running a chain of department stores. Augusta, middle sister Babette, and youngest child and only son Roland have built up a highly successful business over the decades after inheriting from their father, but their plans to make a hefty profit through a top-secret merger are imperiled due to the arrival of their long-lost sister, Sylvia.

Sylvia, the youngest daughter and third of the four children, was their father's favorite child until an argument led to her running away, and no one in the family heard anything from her for decades, until she showed up on the doorstep of the family home and moved in with her siblings. The Ottaway siblings were not particularly pleased to see Sylvia, in part because of the inheritance issues. Their imperious father never bothered to cut his wayward daughter out of the will, so she still stands to inherit a quarter of the business and its profits, even though, as Augusta bitterly points out, it was the three remaining siblings who turned their father's small business into a retail empire with no help from Sylvia. Augusta claims that they tried to get in touch with Sylvia to inform her of her inheritance, though not particularly hard, as they only advertised in a handful of medium-circulation newspapers. While Babette thinks that Sylvia is entitled only to a quarter of the value of the family business at the time their father died, Augusta goes a step further, insisting that the woman claiming to be Sylvia is a shameless impostor. Augusta is convinced that the real Sylvia must have passed away decades earlier, and that somehow the suspect "Sylvia" found out enough about the family to pass herself off in the role. "Sylvia" is a flashy and slatternly woman, wearing a trademark silver Lurex trouser suit and leaving her bedroom mainly for meals and to watch television.

Augusta asks the Hon Con to prove that "Sylvia" is a fraud, and as usual, the Hon Con throws herself wholeheartedly into her investigation. Initial attempts to question "Sylvia" as to details of her family's past are foiled when none of the other three Ottaways can agree on points such as whether one of their uncles drank white port or not, so the Hon Con begins a more detailed investigation. Due to the nature of the problem to be investigated, *WHS* has a much different narrative structure than that of any of Porter's standard whodunits. There are no suspects to be interviewed sequentially, and the people the Hon Con interviews are largely mined for information, rather than being tested to see if they are potential murderers or not.

The Hon Con starts her investigation by attempting to pump the alleged Sylvia for information about her past, but her queries are hampered by "Sylvia's" vagueness and the fact that the three other Ottaway siblings cannot agree on the details of their family's history. A little shaky but inspired reasoning leads to some surprisingly accurate conclusions about "Sylvia's" train transportation to Totterbridge and where "Sylvia" might have been living before coming to town. Her investigation leads to rifling through "Sylvia's" belongings when the family is away at church, and gradually accumulating clues as to where "Sylvia" was living before she came to the Ottaway home. The most important clue is a suitcase stuffed full of money.

Eventually, the Hon Con and Miss Jones track "Sylvia's" past to a seedy seaside resort town, where after a few fruitless questionings at hotels, banks, and a beauty salon, they discover her ties to a local gangster, and the pair must escape the clutches of a criminal organization before returning home to reveal their findings about "Sylvia's" past to the Ottaways. Just as the whole truth (or about as close to the truth as they can ever hope to know) is confessed, an unexpected visitor arrives and sparks a literally explosive situation. After an anticlimactic climax to the confrontation, the Hon Con is stunned to discover that all of her hard work is once again likely to go unappreciated, and the full weight of the law is likely to fall on her rather than the actual criminals.

Assessment

In *WHS*, the Hon Con demonstrates excellent investigative skills and terrible common sense. Her job is to ascertain the truth about a woman's past, and though her approaches are often clumsy and inefficient, it is fair to say that given the logical deductions she uses, her skills as a private investigator have been sharpened substantially over the course of her three previous cases. Unfortunately, her business sense still needs work. The Hon Con leaps at the chance to investigate another case, losing all interest in setting traps for stray cats when Miss Jones delivers the news of Augusta Ottaway's phone call, but with all her enthusiasm, she never gets Augusta to commit to paying her for her services, or even reimbursing her for her expenses. Indeed, Augusta is notoriously cheap, offering the Hon Con a rather pathetic tea of skimpy cucumber sandwiches at their first meeting, and proving to be as slippery as an eel to escape paying for the Hon Con and Miss Jones's travels to other towns as part of the investigation. Most outrageously stingy of all is her meeting with the Hon Con and Miss Jones at an Ottaway's department store tea shop, a tacky place where tea leaves float in the brew, the décor has not been updated in decades, and the waitresses cannot manage to get an order right. As it is her own establishment, Augusta could easily treat the others, but she chooses to make the pair pay for their own food (108). Miss Jones has much better business sense and the Hon Con, being as concerned over the state of her bank account as she is, would do well to take her pal's advice and force all potential clients to sign a binding contract before so much as picking up a magnifying glass at the start of a case.

Throughout the novel, the Hon Con proves herself to have

both a sharper mind than her detractors give her credit for possessing and also that she isn't quite as brilliant as she thinks she is. In the early chapters, while Augusta Ottaway is recruiting the Hon Con to investigate and insisting that the alleged fraud must have been inspired by a television spot featuring the Ottaways, the Hon Con cleverly points out an important fact that none of the Ottaways have detected. If the Ottaways have not made the sordid details of their family history public, how on earth could a con artist have known that there was a Sylvia to impersonate (27)?

In contrast, Miss Jones catches multiple possibilities that have escaped the Hon Con. To cite just one, when the Hon Con discovers "Sylvia's" suitcase filled with money, Miss Jones raises the issue of whether or not the bills might be counterfeit, a possibility that had escaped the Hon Con's notice, though she refuses to admit it (81). As always, the Hon Con never for a second treats Miss Jones as an equal partner in the investigation, assigning Miss Jones time-consuming tasks, and bawling out Miss Jones in front of Augusta Ottaway for making a false conclusion about "Sylvia's" television-watching habits (107-108).

The treatment of Miss Jones in this book is a notable part of a broader theme. More than any other novel in the Hon Con series, Porter uses *WHS* as a means of depicting the lasting class system in England, which since the Second World War has warped into something less elegant yet just as rigid as what it was in the first half of the twentieth century. Miss Jones's treatment represents the fact that domestic servants are considered lower classes. While the other inhabitants of Totterbridge may not be sure of the exact status of her relationship with the Hon Con, they do know that Miss Jones performs most of the housework, and the Hon Con has all the money, which relegates poor Miss Jones to the lower levels of the caste system. On multiple occasions, Augusta Ottaway decries the current state of the servant class to the Hon Con, on occasion deliberately lumping Miss Jones in with the rest of the rabble of domestic service, and referring to Miss Jones as "little Miss– er– What's-her-name" (12, 34, 87). The Hon Con only occasionally rises to the defense of her friend. At their ill-fated tea, Augusta makes it clear that she views Miss Jones as a social inferior by forcing objects upon her to clear away from the table (101).

Turnabout is fair play, and the Hon Con in turn sees the Ottaways as being a few rungs below her on the social ladder, for despite their significant wealth, they are in trade, and though Porter doesn't spell out the reasoning for this derisive attitude, it is clear that the Hon Con feels that there is something uncouth about making a living by hawking goods to the masses. Porter's omniscient narrator notes that the Ottaways "were an old and extremely respectable family but they suffered from one serious disability: they were in trade" (9). Other characters demonstrate the lengths that one will go to in an attempt to rise up in the world, like a bank manager who spent a significant sum of money getting elocution lessons to lose his Scottish brogue in order to fit in better in England (112). There's also the issue of race prejudice, as some major characters accept certain dismissive and false stereotypes towards some black individuals. In one case, a black character plays into stereotypes as a means of annoying the Hon Con, avoiding answering her questions directly and affecting a caricatured foolish demeanor in order to be left alone. The character in this scene is far more intelligent than he portrays himself as being, as he is a graduate student feigning foolishness as his own private joke (51-52).

Not all the characters on the lower rungs of the social ladder accept the social status that is imposed upon them. Annie, the Ottaways' sullen maid, upon seeing the Hon Con wearing one of her grandfather's old suits, tells her she looks "like a superannuated rat-catcher" (34). Luckily for her, the Hon Con unhesitatingly accepts the comment as a great compliment. As the Ottaways' saucy maid's derisive behavior illustrates, the social system has been shaken up over the past few decades, and there are many who used to be on the bottom who no longer feel that they owe their so-called superiors any respect, but for those who still do believe in the system, the arbitrary lines that make one sort of people superior to another may have shifted, but they are still there.

The Ottaways embody a certain coarseness that may be representative of character defects affecting a broader segment of society. All of the Ottaways are essentially overgrown children. Augusta is a pushy elder sister, bossing her siblings and demanding respect for her position while doing nothing to earn genuine moral superiority or be likeable. Babette is very much a spoilt child, pouting and sulking whenever she doesn't get her way or is chastised. Roland acts like a timid little boy, fading into the background and almost never asserting himself. Finally, "Sylvia" behaves like an annoying teenager, lounging about in her bedroom, sneering at her siblings' happy memories, and affecting an air of urbane superiority. They care mainly about money, are horrified at the prospect that a scandal may affect their wealth, and are willing to lie and withhold the truth in order to get the better end of a business deal, saying that hiding damaging information from business partners is "life" (24). When they go to church, it's only to pray for record sales, and their employees who attend the service in order to be seen by their bosses bow and scrape in front of them, and the Ottaways bask in the power of their social position (61, 73-75).

Other than a gangster who models himself after Edward G. Robinson, the Ottaways are the most thoroughly developed characters in the book, aside from our heroines, whose characterizations are further deepened. There are a couple of scenes which reveal the Hon Con's attraction to lovely younger women. A brief line reveals that the Hon Con's romantic predilections are no secret in the village. In one scene, Miss Jones reveals that she always knocks on the door of the Hon Con's private gymnasium after one time when she walked in while the Hon Con was practicing her fencing and Miss Jones came close to losing an eye. There is a brief flashback to the Hon Con's disastrous tenure on the local fencing team, when she attempted to duel the male captain over the attentions of "a completely worthless little minx of a troublemaker called Jasmin McSparran" (79). (It is unclear whether the deprecatory words are those of the omniscient narrator or if the omniscient narrator is reading Miss Jones's mind and reporting her thoughts.) In another scene, the Hon Con notes that the woman calling herself Sylvia has no physical attraction for her because she's too old (37). In the middle of their investigation, the Hon Con is overcome with lust at the sight of a comely bank teller, making no attempt to disguise her swelling passion from Miss Jones, who is standing right beside her (111).

There's a slip-up in Porter's writing early in the book. In the Hon Con's first conversation with Augusta, early in the scene Augusta mentions the stress arising from the upcoming merger (15). Several pages later, when Augusta explains why she's asking for the Hon Con to be extremely hush-hush with her investigation, she explains the delicate nature of the merger negotiations, as if she has never referenced them before that moment (23). This was probably simply an error on Porter's part that was never caught by the editors and is in no way a hidden clue or deliberate red herring.

While the ending is clearly unsatisfactory to those fans who are rooting to see the Hon Con finally get the recognition she deserves for all of her hard work and pluck, a little reasoning indicates that if the Hon Con were only to relax her grip on her wallet and spring for competent legal counsel, she might be vindicated. A little forensic examination regarding fingerprints on certain objects would give the lie to certain characters' insistence that they did not believe they were in any danger, and if the Hon Con were really determined to seek out some malicious vengeance, she could ask the income tax authorities to look into "Sylvia's" suitcase full of cash. As *MHM* shows, the Hon Con has been able to extricate herself out of a sticky legal situation before with a little judicious hiring of professional help, so it is possible that the Ottaway case wrapped up on a much pleasanter note than is recorded in the book. Unfortunately, no clarification is provided in the next book, *CBC*. In any case, by this point in her career, the Hon Con has developed into a tenacious, effective, but by no means prudent sleuth. It is a shame that she had only one more recorded case left in her career.

Chapter Twenty: The Cart Before the Crime (1979)

The Plot

In the Hon Con's final appearance, she is given busy work in order to keep her out of the way of a local committee, but in a supreme irony, an attempt to fob her off on a meaningless investigation turns into the most consequential case of her career.

As the novel opens, Miss Jones is cornered by the women of a committee that has been recently formed to prepare for the coming of a Very Important Royal Personage (VIRP), who will be visiting their village as part of a general tour. A big public presentation is being planned, and several prominent women are all jostling to gain control over the committee's direction and to shape the events honoring the VIRP into their own preferred images. Every decision is controversial and potentially inflammatory, but there is one point where all the women of the committee disagree: the Hon Con must be kept out of the preparations. As a member of the local aristocracy, the Hon Con cannot be denied admittance into the planning committee—her rank precludes her exclusion—but everybody, even Miss Jones, knows that if the Hon Con were to wrest control of planning for the VIRP's visit, the results could be disastrous.

Therefore, the other members of the planning committee order poor Miss Jones to find a way to keep the Hon Con from getting too involved with VIRP-related activities for several months, and everybody agrees that the best way to distract her is to get her obsessed with an investigation. However, there is never a mysterious murder or a jewel robbery or anything like that when one really needs it, and the best that Miss Jones can do is to make the Hon Con wonder why a prominent local couple is planning to sell the family home.

It is not the most compelling question, but the Hon Con is very concerned that the "wrong sort" of people will move into the neighborhood and turn that prime piece of real estate into a nasty eyesore or some sort of moral blemish on the village. The owners refuse to provide her with any details, so driven partly by curiosity and mostly by sheer bloody-mindedness, the Hon Con continues to investigate the estate agents behind the sale, all in an attempt to find out just who is purchasing a massive house with a moat around it. Along the way, the Hon Con and Miss Jones investigate by questioning office staff, borrowing a local dog to walk in order to justify a stakeout, and come across a former smut king attempting to go legitimate.

The investigation is punctuated by the Hon Con's efforts to contribute to the festivities for the VIRP's visit, mostly in the form of trying to build a horse-drawn carriage, despite having no carpentry skills. In the end, the Hon Con is compelled by her own lack of ability to settle for making a sedan chair, and enlisting a skilled craftsman to assist her. She still insists on playing a role in carrying the VIRP around, and her presence on the scene soon alerts her to a looming danger that only she can thwart.

Pretty much every reader will realize long before the Hon Con that her investigation is actually tied into a threat against the VIRP, and at the last second, the Hon Con puts together the pieces and saves the VIRP. Unfortunately for the Hon Con, as usual, the Hon Con's unrestrained behavior provokes the police to use her as a scapegoat for their own shortcomings. That means that the Hon Con is denied the knighthood she feels she deserves for her cleverness and heroism, and the series ends on a bitter note.

Assessment

The actual mystery in *CBC* is fairly slight, as it should be obvious to all readers that if anything untoward is being plotted, the VIRP will be the clear target. The reader is therefore way ahead of the characters in the book, as the savvy reader will identify the villains well before the ending, and once the bad guys are spotted, it is very clear what is being planned and how it is supposed to go into effect. It is therefore the slightest of the Hon Con novels, as it is not really a whodunnit, whydunnit or even a howdunnit, not when it's so easy to figure out what happening. Simultaneously, one cannot really blame the Hon Con for being so slow to piece everything together, for while the readers know that they are following the narrative of a crime novel, the Hon Con does not believe she is inquiring into anything more dangerous than a simple real estate sale. As the villains' evil plot will logically be put into place during the festivities, it is clear that the whole book is simply leading up to the climactic scene, and the only questions are when the Hon Con will piece everything together and how successful she will be in saving the situation.

While *CBC* is a reasonably simple to unravel mystery, which certainly makes it the weakest in the series, and perhaps the weakest in Porter's oeuvre altogether, that does not mean that the book is not worth reading. While the plotting and clueing are not up to Porter's usual standard, the Hon Con and Miss Jones are still delightful to read about, as they remain an entertainingly mismatched comic team.

As there are no real criminal suspects in the Hon Con's investigation, most of the interviewees lack the possibility that they might be dangerous beneath their pleasant exteriors, as is the case in the murder mysteries, so they are less memorable. Perhaps the most notable new character is Manny Schnapper, a breezy, sleazy fellow who, after making his fortune in pornography and sensual entertainment, has decided to redirect the focus of his business to exploit more a wholesome subject: the commoditization of religion. Schnapper plans to make a bundle off of a secular society's interest in spiritual matters, charging for tours of convents and monasteries. This would help the perpetually cash-strapped religious orders make ends meet, and Schnapper would get a nice cut of the proceeds. The Hon Con is impressed by this plan to open up religious life to spectators, while Miss Jones, ever the clergyman's daughter, is horrified. Porter, as always, respects religion while tweaking the noses of those who might debase the practice of faith by trying to make a buck off of it.

CBC shows just how much the Hon Con is a pariah in Totterbridge. She enjoys a certain level of respect that she can never lose due to her wealth and title, but aside from Miss

Jones, hardly anyone in town wants to spend any time with her. Her reputation for taking charge and then making a total mess of things is common knowledge, which is why the other women planning for the VIRP's visit are devoting most of their time to freezing the Hon Con out and distracting her with supposed wild goose chases (and using the rest of their time to play "Queen of the Hill" metaphorically in attempts to exert more and more control and influence over the planning committee). The Hon Con has become a grotesque joke in her village, a destructive annoyance who is ignored or sidelined whenever possible. Fortunately, the Hon Con, so worldly in many other ways, is naïvely unaware of just how frustrated the rest of the community is by her domineering manner that generally leads to disaster.

It stands to reason that the Hon Con would be utterly lost without the support and assistance of her sole faithful companion. It is very subtly written, but a scene where Miss Jones reflects on her life if the Hon Con were to pass away provides a tragic possibility for her character if one thinks about it in depth. For the first time, Porter raises the question, what will happen if the Hon Con were to die? It's not spelled out thoroughly, but as the daughter of an earl, the Hon Con inherited a substantial income. Many members of the aristocracy don't inherit their money outright, and it's certainly possible that the Hon Con has no control over who gets her wealth when she dies. It will likely pass on to some other family member, possibly a cousin. Miss Jones might receive a little legacy, but given her backup plan to find another friend to serve as a housekeeper for (a contingency plan that is forever dashed due to Miss Jones' unwilling involvement in the Hon Con's schemes), Miss Jones might be left destitute and homeless with the death of the Hon Con (126-127). It is a fate that befalls many women in her position. Agatha Christie made a point of illustrating the fate that befalls elderly single women with no children who worked in domestic service in *Five Little Pigs* and *The Labors of Hercules*. The women had nothing to look forward to but a lonely old age in a single drafty room with barely enough to eat. Given the changes in government assistance over forty years, Miss Jones would have food and shelter, but Porter made a point of savaging the situation senior citizens faced when they depend on the government in "Dover Without Perks." In that story, an elderly woman was moved away from all of her friends and home, and placed in a run-down flat miles away from all she knew "for her own good." Life was essentially solitary confinement for these women living on skimpy pensions with nothing but a television for company. Knowing that she might lose all control over her future, it is no wonder why Miss Jones keeps pushing salads on the Hon Con.

Miss Jones may be looking after the Hon Con's health, but it is revealed in *CBC* that the Hon Con, previously only shown to flirt with and secretly lust after young women, has had at least one sexual relationship with another woman. Rita Aizelewood, an employee at a realtor's office, and the Hon Con had a brief but passionate fling sometime earlier when they were badminton partners (the Hon Con was kicked out of the local badminton club when she smashed her racquet over someone else's head in a fit of pique), and now Rita is engaged to a man. Needing Rita's assistance in gathering information on the local real estate transaction, the Hon Con shamelessly blackmails her ex-lover. The Hon Con caps off her extortion pitch by referencing Rita's fiancé and threateningly remarking,

"I might even be able to give him a few tips" (40). The Hon Con gets the information she needs, but she also makes an enemy of her former paramour (38-42).

There is one more point that indicates that the Hon Con and Miss Jones are not in a romantic relationship. While the Hon Con is certainly blackmailing Rita, Rita never takes it into her head to threaten to tell Miss Jones about their affair. Perhaps it never crosses her mind to fight fire with fire, and perhaps Rita believes that in a confrontation of mutually assured destruction she would have much more to lose, but it also indicates that the Hon Con really has nothing to fear regarding Miss Jones learning about her relationships with other women. As mentioned earlier, Miss Jones may be economically bound to the Hon Con, but as shown in the previous four novels, Miss Jones can make life very uncomfortable for the Hon Con if she's displeased, without fear of being fired and expelled from the household. Many lines of dialogue and scenes can still be interpreted in multiple ways, so after five novels, the exact relationship between the pair remains deliberately ambiguous, though with each passing book, there is increasing evidence that though the two are extremely close, their bond is not romantic. No matter what the actual state of their connection is, it can be said for certain that Miss Jones is the Hon Con's only real friend, and Miss Jones is extremely loyal, even if the Hon Con doesn't always treat Miss Jones with the consideration that she deserves.

(Note: Oblique spoilers follow)

While Dover's career ended with him blackmailing his way to a promotion, the Hon Con's name is besmirched in her final appearance by a system desperate to protect its own reputation by smearing the name of the one person responsible for preventing a disastrous situation. As the Hon Con herself declares, she ought to be receiving a knighthood (no damehood for her, she wants the masculine title) for her services, declaring "It's a knighthood or nothing as far as I'm concerned" (164). This proves to be wishful thinking on her part. Just like in *RCSC*, giving the Hon Con her due would mean that the authorities would have to admit to gross negligence and incompetence, and they refuse to call the integrity of the system into question. Therefore, it is deemed to be better to focus on the heroine's mistakes rather than her achievements, for humiliating the Hon Con is preferable to those in positions of power than it would be for the career bureaucrats running the country to get a well-deserved black eye.

As in the final Dover novel, *DBB*, the ending shows how the British establishment's desire to maintain the semblance of propriety and the confidence of the citizenry is given precedence over justice and truth. As usual, the reader has to look between the lines to extract this subtext, because Porter never let editorializing get in the way of an entertaining mystery.

The slightness of the plotting of *CBC* may illustrate that Porter was growing tired of writing mysteries and that she was ready to retire from her second career. The Hon Con would never get another chance to get the credit she deserved for her crimefighting efforts, and Porter would only produce one last Dover novel before covering her mystery-writing typewriter. Fans can understandably be disappointed that Porter did not have the inclination or inspiration to produce any more crime novels for the last decade of her life.

IV

Part Four

Adaptations of Porter's Work

Chapter Twenty-One: Dover on TV and Radio

Despite the rich material and humor in Porter's work, very little of it has been adapted. There are no feature films based on her work, and only one television adaptation, though there are five popular BBC radio plays based on the Dover mysteries and one original Dover audio drama that have helped to keep Porter's work in the public eye and attract new fans.

The Television Adaptation

Dover and the Deadly Poison Pen Letters (1968)

The hour-long television anthology series *Detective* adapted numerous classic and lesser-known mysteries for viewers at home. Stories by Sir Arthur Conan Doyle, G.K. Chesterton, Anthony Berkeley, Edgar Allan Poe, along with those of dozens of less famous writers, were dramatized. According to the Internet Movie Database, on May 24th, 1968, Porter's *D3* was retitled *Dover and the Deadly Poison Pen Letters* and was broadcast as the second episode of the second season (Dover and the Deadly Poison Pen Letters). Paul Dawkins played

Dover, and James Cosmo took on the role of MacGregor.

No recording of *DDPPL* is readily available, so the production cannot be critiqued or described. As fans of classic *Doctor Who* are all too well aware, during the 1960s, the BBC was not very scrupulous in preserving its broadcasts for posterity. Only about half of the filmed episodes of *Detective* survived, and the rest are believed lost (Dover and the Deadly Poison Pen Letters). It is not clear whether *DDPPL* was preserved, but as of this writing, it is not available on VHS, DVD, or streaming.

The Radio Plays

Dover Goes to Pott

All of Paul Mendelson's Dover radio plays open with an exasperated and disheartened MacGregor tapping away at a typewriter, begging his superiors to give him a transfer away from Dover. The account of the case is provided through flashbacks as MacGregor writes his report in order to prove to his superiors just how impossible Dover is to work with, and to justify the transfer.

Each episode opens with MacGregor identifying which number application for transfer he is writing, but the first and the last episodes do not provide the date that MacGregor is writing his report. *DGP* is undated, but MacGregor declares that this is his twenty-third application for transfer. On occasion, MacGregor's narration provides a verbal bridge between scenes, and each episode ends with MacGregor desperately pleading for his bosses to have mercy and terminate his partnership with Dover.

DGP is a pretty faithful adaptation to the book, aside

from some necessary abridgements for time. One of the biggest changes comes at the end, as the fate of the killer is never revealed in the novel, whereas in the radio adaptation MacGregor explains the exact sentence the killer received (*Dover Goes to Pott* (radio adaptation)).

All of the Dover radio plays are just under one hour long, with the exception of *DSG* which is only forty-five minutes in length. All episodes feature Kenneth Cranham as Dover and Stuart McQuarrie as MacGregor.

Dover and the Sleeping Beauty

DSB is the most heavily changed radio adaptation from the original source material. In the opening, MacGregor states that he is writing this on November 2, 1966, and this is his one hundred forty-second application for transfer. As the title indicates, this adaptation is mostly based on *D2*, though a subplot from *IMD* has been incorporated into the storyline.

The basic premise of the mystery remains the same. The alterations range from minor character changes to major plot restructuring. When Dover is asked about his religious beliefs in the book, he professes to be a Methodist. In the radio play, when questioned about his religious affiliation, Dover replies with a wholly secular "I believe in law, truth, and justice, and that right will always prevail" (*Dover and the Sleeping Beauty*). This pronouncement is preceded by a bitter laugh by MacGregor immediately after the local police officer asks the question, and this statement of faith seems to clash with Dover's general disinterest in investigations, unless his total laziness is viewed as an absolute faith that a *deus ex machina* will right all wrongs. Indeed, the Protestant/Catholic feuding, so central to the book, is either heavily watered down or excised completely from the radio play.

The biggest changes are connected with the order of events. In the book, it is revealed about two-thirds of the way through that the shooter and the smotherer are two separate people, and the smotherer's relationship with the victim is uncovered halfway through the book, and the identity of the smotherer is revealed at the same time it is made clear that the smotherer is not responsible for the shooting. Dover's uncharacteristic emotional connection to the case is played down, and the smotherer in the radio play is shown to be in severe mental distress, but does not fall into full-fledged insanity as in the book. At the end of the novel, the shooter confesses while Dover is accusing the wrong person, and is arrested soon afterwards. It is revealed that the shooter was having an affair with the person Dover was falsely accusing (rather than just an unrequited crush), and that the victim was planning to reveal it to the world.

The investigation in the radio play reverses the order of several events. In the book, the shooter confesses late in the play while Dover is accusing the wrong person, but in the radio play, the shooter has kept the gun instead of disposing of it, and is only arrested after a shoot-out, in the middle of which the shooter denies being involved in the smothering. In the book, it is the victim who had an affair with the wrongly accused character, and the shooter shot the victim out of jealousy. In the closing minutes of the radio play, after the shooter is taken into custody, Dover pieces together the rest of the puzzle without sharing his suspicions with MacGregor, and accuses the smotherer at the victim's funeral. After being taxed with the truth, the smotherer confesses, but Dover then reveals the true connection between the victim and the smotherer, leading to an emotional breakdown in the graveyard. Dover deduced the details of the connection by observing an odd bit of phrasing in an earlier conversation.

The other change is a subplot involving Dover being the guest of Chief Constable Muckle during his investigation. In the book, Dover's lodgings at the Station Hotel are not given much attention, but the radio play transplants the storyline from *IMD* and turns it into a major subplot. Instead of staying with a pair of impoverished aristocratic siblings who eat skimpy vegetarian meals for reasons of economics and personal taste, as in *IMD*, the Muckle family members are vegetarians out of moral principle. While Lady Priscilla Crouch was a terrible cook, Dover comes to find Mrs. Muckle's meatless meals quite tasty, and when eating in a restaurant, tries other vegetarian foods because he finds he does not feel nearly as tired after consuming his fill of them. Dover's flirtation with vegetarianism ends on the ride home, after he devours some Scotch eggs with gusto, afterwards desiring a lettuce leaf not for sustenance, but as a napkin to wipe away the crumbs. Additionally, instead of a phrase chanted by a random child inspiring Dover to realize the solution, it is the Muckles' poetry-loving daughter who provides Dover with the clue for the motive behind the smotherer's attack.

Dover and the Claret Tappers

The narrative flashes forward a decade to February 25th, 1976, and MacGregor is filling out his two hundred fifty-first application for transfer. At that rate, MacGregor has been begging for the dissolution of his partnership with Dover a little less often than once a month for ten years. This adaptation of *Dover and the Claret Tappers* hews fairly closely to the source material, until the final act.

In the original novel, MacGregor deduces the Claret Tappers' plan himself, and Dover misses the final hunt for the kidnapping gang due to his gastrointestinal distress. MacGregor then explains what happens to him at the end, and Dover sulks because he hasn't been rewarded for his contribution to rescuing the Prime Minister's grandson. In the adaptation, Dover pieces together the clues on his own (though MacGregor insists he already made the deductions himself and that Dover denies him any chance at the limelight), and goes to rescue the baby himself after the other police track down the kidnappers' location, though MacGregor follows him without Dover being aware of it until the last second. MacGregor tags along out of resentfulness, as he is sick of Dover withholding important information from him. In the epilogue, it is revealed that Dover might have received a medal for his help in capturing the villains, but someone leaked the fact that Dover was trapped in a lavatory for a day and a half during his kidnapping to the *Daily Mail*. The headline refers to Dover as "Toilet Cop" and "Inspector Dandruff," due to the copious amounts of Dover's dead scalp cells found in the bathroom. Though Dover is given credit for solving the case, the powers that be declare that the *Daily Mail* story brings ridicule to the force, so Dover is denied a promotion or any other honor for the sake of Scotland Yard's self-image. Dover believes that MacGregor is responsible for this vindictive leak, and he is correct, though MacGregor does not take credit for this bit of malicious sabotage.

Dover Beats the Band

This adventure is dated March 14th, 1976, and MacGregor is filing his two hundred ninety-fourth application for transfer.

This is probably a flaw, because based on the information in *DCT*, that would mean that MacGregor filed forty-three transfer applications in eighteen days (1976 was a leap year), or over two a day, which seems excessive even for him.

DBB is very faithful to the original source material, with a few minor alterations. In the book, Dover expresses sympathy for the fascist organization's racist goals, and the ranking officer of Special Branch concurs. In the radio adaptation, after hearing that the fascists want to "Send all the blacks home, expel the Jews, restore hanging, and repeal equal rights for women," Dover replies with a disgusted, "Terrible." After a moment's reflection, he qualifies this statement and adds, "I'm in favor of the last two meself, actually" (*Dover Beats the Band* (Radio play)).

The other major change is that in the closing scene, where Dover shows up at MacGregor's home early in the morning to reveal his solution to the mystery. At the end, it's revealed that MacGregor has spent the night with their driver, Elvira. Dover disapprovingly warns him against that sort of exertion, saying, "Saps your brain, you know. That's why my mind's sharp as a tack. Put it all down to Mrs. Dover and her long flannel nighties" (*Dover Beats the Band* (Radio play)).

Dover and the Unkindest Cut of All

This adaptation is very close to the original source material. It is set on November 21st, 1976, and it is MacGregor's three hundred twenty-first application for transfer. With a total of twenty-seven applications over the course of more than nine months, MacGregor's rate of complaint is a bit more reasonable. In this episode, Dover is still a Detective Chief Inspector, despite being promoted to Detective Superintendent at the end of *DBB*. Either this is an oversight, or Dover was demoted, which is unlikely since he received his promotion in order to buy his silence.

There are few significant changes to the narrative, although it is made clear at the end of the radio play that one mysterious death remains officially unsolved as no one believes Dover's solution (which happens to be the truth), and MacGregor tells his superiors he will continue to follow leads that the listener knows will take him down a false path.

Dover and the Smoking Gun

In this original story by Paul Mendelson, listeners learn that MacGregor is now on his eight hundred sixty-third application for transfer, though no clue is given as to how much time has passed since *Dover and the Unkindest Cut of All*. It cannot be that long, as MacGregor still calls himself a "young police officer." One of the reasons for MacGregor's bachelorhood is revealed, as it is shown that MacGregor has long carried a torch for a woman who broke up with him years earlier and married a hypnotherapist. This lost love has been killed in a car crash, and MacGregor suspects murder, despite the fact that her death was officially ruled an accident. MacGregor rushes back to his hometown in Scotland for the funeral and an unofficial investigation, and after going AWOL, Dover (still sporting a DCI title for some reason) is ordered up to Scotland to bring MacGregor home.

Upon arrival, Dover demands free room and board at the MacGregor family home. MacGregor's mother is deceased, and MacGregor's father is a dour man who disapproves of drinking, smoking, and Dover in general. The investigation shows that MacGregor's ex-girlfriend was an actress set to star in a musical production of *Macbeth*, and her relationship with her arrogant husband was strained. As revelations of an affair leak, and the deceased's desperation to become a mother is uncovered, the detectives interview the play's director, other villagers, and a wannabe actress connected to the dead woman. Dover prevents another murder on the set of the show and decides to see if the recently widowed hypnotherapist can help him quit smoking.

For once, it is MacGregor who believes the husband is guilty and Dover is unconvinced of his guilt. There are a couple of seconds where Dover exhibits uncharacteristic sympathy for MacGregor when he realizes that his subordinate has been in love with this woman all this time, but the moment quickly fades. After an investigation where Dover ruffles enough feathers to provoke another call for a Scottish secession from the United Kingdom, Dover manages to piece the clues together, realizes how the murder was actually committed, and who did it. In the climactic scene, Dover, MacGregor, and an unlikely ally confront the killer and must both obtain a confession and prevent a suicide.

This is the only episode not to end with a voiceover from MacGregor wrapping up his transfer request. Instead, MacGregor's father expresses incredulity that his son has managed to work with Dover for so long, and MacGregor desperately declares that the authorities must accept his most recent transfer request. Upon hearing this, Dover happily replies that there is no chance of that, not when no other detective at Scotland Yard will work with him.

Conclusion: Porter's Legacy

P orter wrote Golden Age-style mysteries set in a world cast out of base metal. Her books had the good-natured light heart that was present in many early twentieth-century thrillers, along with the fair play clueing of the Golden Age, while filling her books with the disillusioned and often shabby atmosphere of the culture of her day.

Porter has always had a cult following rather than widespread acclaim and fame, though her work is beloved by her fans. Porter's work has frequently suffered from going out of print, only to be brought back a few years later by a different publisher. Since around the time of Porter's death, at least three different businesses have printed her works. Her fans have remembered her work, and new fans have discovered her, often due in part to the BBC radio adaptations.

Most authors fade away into obscurity and are forgotten not long after their deaths, but Porter's fans have made a valiant effort to raise public awareness of her work. Porter has always thrived thanks to her niche appeal, but is there any chance that over thirty years after her death, she could make inroads into the broader popular culture? There seems to be only one way that long-awaited success could be achieved, and that is through adaptations of her work. A Dover television series, with the right casting and strong scripts, has the potential to become a substantial hit, especially for fans of clever mysteries and raucous humor. Likewise, a skilled female comedy team could make for highly entertaining viewing on a television series based on the Hon Con novels. There are a handful of potential hazards to such an undertaking. Porter's sense of humor is what makes her books work, yet her style and tone are challenging to mimic, and even more dangerously, some production teams might decide to tone down the exuberant comedy that has won Porter loyal fans, thereby stripping away her strongest asset and potentially reworking the books into nothing more than a plain, paint-by-numbers production that is exactly like dozens of other uninspired crime television series.

It is an axiom in many mystery fiction circles that once an author dies, that writer's oeuvre starts dying. Many of the most acclaimed and successful crime novelists of the twentieth century faded away into obscurity and fell out of print within a decade or two after their deaths, their once-household names now known only by devotees of the genre, their books available for sale only in battered condition from used booksellers. There are several exceptions to the rule, such as Agatha Christie and Arthur Conan Doyle. Forty years after Porter's death, and two generations since she stopped writing mysteries, Porter is in danger of becoming a footnote in the history of mystery fiction, but with the right push into popular culture and if a publisher brings back her entire oeuvre (at least in e-book form), there's a real possibility of rediscovery. In the meantime, Porter's books are being used to make the world she so wittily criticized a better place. The Farrago e-book editions of the Dover novels, newly re-released in 2020, donate the royalties to the registered charity The Friends of Friendless Churches, which protects and preserves decommissioned religious buildings in England and Wales, thereby saving their cultural and historical value. These donations are made possible through the kindness of the Literary Estate of Joyce Porter.

Only time will tell if a Porter revival will take off and make Dover, Eddie Brown, and the Hon Con popular culture figures on a par with Sherlock Holmes, Hercule Poirot, Miss Marple, Father Brown, and Perry Mason. It is to be hoped that this study will have played a role in helping Porter to earn the recognition and respect she deserves.

Works Cited

Chesterton, G.K. *The Man Who Knew Too Much*. U.S.A.: Harper & Brothers, 1922. *Google Books*. Web. 19 February 2020.

Christie, Agatha. *Miss Marple: The Complete Short Stories*. New York: HarperCollins Publishers, 2011. Print.

Christie, Agatha. *The Moving Finger*. New York: Harper-Collins Publishers, 2011. Print.

"Currency Converter." https://www.xe.com/currencyconverter/convert/?Amount=58%2C910.03&From=GBP&To=USD. XE.com Inc., 2020. Web. 19 February 2020.

"Dover and the Deadly Poison Pen Letters." https://www.imdb.com/title/tt0558789/?ref_=ttep_ep2. Imdb, n.d. Web. 19 February 2020.

"Inflation Calculator– British Pound." https://www.inflationtool.com/british-pound?amount=4000&year1=1968&year2=2019. Inflation Tool, 2020. Web. 19 February 2020.

"Joyce Porter." https://en.wikipedia.org/wiki/Joyce_Porter. Wikipedia, 29 January 2020. Web. 19 February 2020.

Mendelson, Paul. "Dover and the Claret Tappers." BBC Radio 4. MP3.

Mendelson, Paul. "Dover and the Sleeping Beauty." BBC Radio 4. MP3.

Mendelson, Paul. "Dover and the Smoking Gun." BBC Radio 4. MP3.

Mendelson, Paul. "Dover and the Unkindest Cut of All."

BBC Radio 4. MP3.

Mendelson, Paul. "Dover Beats the Band." BBC Radio 4. MP3.

Mendelson, Paul. "Dover Goes to Pott." BBC Radio 4. MP3.

Myre, Greg. "Stanislav Petrov, 'The Man Who Saved The World,' Dies At 77." https://www.npr.org/sections/thetwo-way/2017/09/18/551792129/stanislav-petrov-the-man-who-saved-the-world-dies-at-77. NPR, 18 September 2017. Web. 19 February 2020.

Porter, Joyce. *The Cart Before the Crime*. U.K.: Bello, 2013. Print.

Porter, Joyce. *The Chinks in the Curtain*. New York: Charles Scribner's Sons. 1966. Print.

Porter, Joyce. *Dover: The Collected Short Stories*. Woodstock, Vermont: Foul Play Press, 1995. Print.

Porter, Joyce. *Dover Beats the Band*. Woodstock, Vermont: Foul Play Press, 19913. Print.

Porter, Joyce. *Dead Easy for Dover*. Woodstock, Vermont: Foul Play Press, 1991. Print.

Porter, Joyce. *Dover and the Claret Tappers*. Woodstock, Vermont: Foul Play Press, 1992. Print.

Porter, Joyce. *Dover and the Unkindest Cut of All*. Woodstock, Vermont: Foul Play Press, 1990. Print.

Porter, Joyce. *Dover and the Unkindest Cut of All*. U.K.: Farrago, 2019. Kindle edition. 18 February 2020.

Porter, Joyce. *Dover Goes to Pott*. Woodstock, Vermont: Foul Play Press, 1990. Print.

Porter, Joyce. *Dover Goes to Pott*. U.K.: Farrago, 2019. Kindle edition. 18 February 2020.

Porter, Joyce. *Dover One*. Woodstock, Vermont: Foul Play Press, 1989. Print.

Porter, Joyce. *Dover One*. U.K.: Farrago, 2019. Kindle edition. 18 February 2020.

Porter, Joyce. *Dover Strikes Again*. Woodstock, Vermont: Foul Play Press, 1991. Print.

Porter, Joyce. *Dover Strikes Again*. U.K.: Farrago, 2020. Kindle edition. 18 February 2020.

Porter, Joyce. *Dover Three*. Woodstock, Vermont: Foul Play Press, 1989. Print.

Porter, Joyce. *Dover Three*. U.K.: Farrago, 2019. Kindle edition. 18 February 2020.

Porter, Joyce. *Dover Two*. Woodstock, Vermont: Foul Play Press, 1989. Print.

Porter, Joyce. *Dover Two*. U.K.: Farrago, 2019. Kindle edition. 18 February 2020.

Porter, Joyce. *It's Murder with Dover*. Woodstock, Vermont: Foul Play Press, 1992. Print.

Porter, Joyce. *It's Murder with Dover*. U.K.: Farrago, 2020. Kindle edition. 18 February 2020.

Porter, Joyce. *A Meddler and Her Murder*. Chicago: Academy Chicago Publishers, 2005. Print.

Porter, Joyce. *Neither a Candle Nor a Pitchfork*. New York: McCall Publishing Co., 1970. Print.

Porter, Joyce. *Only with a Bargepole*. U.S.A.: David McKay Company/Ives Washburn, 1974. Print.

Porter, Joyce. *The Package Included Murder*. Great Britain: Black Dagger Crime, 2001. Print.

Porter, Joyce. *Rather a Common Sort of Crime*. New York: McCall Publishing Co., 1970. Print.

Porter, Joyce. *Sour Cream with Everything*. New York: Charles Scribner's Sons. 1966. Print.

Porter, Joyce. *Who the Heck is Sylvia?* London: Weidenfeld

& Nicholson, 1977. Print.

Symons, Julian. *Bloody Murder: From the Detective Story to the Crime Novel: A History, 3rd Revised Edition.* New York: Mysterious Press, 1992. Print.

A Note from the Author

This book is written in the hopes that it will help Joyce Porter gain the audience she deserves, and that future readers of Porter's works will enjoy her books as much as I do.

Acknowledgements

Special thanks to Shawn Reilly Simmons, Verena Rose, and Harriette Sackler for believing in this project. Further thanks to Martin Edwards for providing the recommendation that led to publication, and additional thanks to Patrick Ohl for encouraging me to write a book on Joyce Porter.

About the Author

Chris Chan is a writer, educator and historian. He works as a researcher and "International Goodwill Ambassador" for Agatha Christie Ltd. His true crime articles, reviews, and short fiction have appeared (or will soon appear) in *The Strand*, *The Wisconsin Magazine of History*, *Mystery Weekly*, *Gilbert!*, *Nerd HQ*, Akashic Books' Mondays are Murder webseries, *The Baker Street Journal*, *The MX Book of New Sherlock Holmes Stories*, *Masthead: The Best New England Crime Stories*, *Sherlock Holmes Mystery Magazine*, and multiple Belanger Books anthologies. He is the creator of the Funderburke mysteries, a series featuring a private investigator who works for a school and helps students during times of crisis.The Funderburke short story "The Six-Year-Old Serial Killer" was nominated for a Derringer Award. His first book, *Sherlock & Irene: The Secret Truth Behind "A Scandal in Bohemia,"* was published in 2020 by MX Publishing.

CPSIA information can be obtained
at www.ICGtesting.com
Printed in the USA
LVHW011602151022
730779LV00003B/245